SELF-PUBLISHING
— FROM —
SCRATCH

SELF-PUBLISHING
— FROM —
SCRATCH

A PRACTICAL GUIDE FOR AUTHORS TO
PUBLISH SUCCESSFULLY WITH
INSIGHTS FOR BLACK VOICES

KEYIMANI ALFORD

KW

**KEYWORDS
UNLOCKED**

ISBN (Hardcover): 979-8-9990953-2-9
ISBN (Paperback): 979-8-9990953-4-3
ISBN (eBook): 979-8-9990953-3-6

Printed in the United States of America.

Published by Keywords Unlocked Publishers
6969 N. Port Washington Road, Suite B150, PMB #1025
Glendale, Wisconsin 53217
keywordsunlockedllc@gmail.com

For information, visit: www.keywordsunlocked.com

WHAT READERS ARE SAYING

I'm blown away by Self-Publishing from Scratch, your personal journey and cultural insights are a game-changer for Black writers like me. – **Beta Reader**

I really commend you for your brave work. The novel is one of the best and I appreciate you for sharing your opinion with others. – **Beta Reader**

This book's a real gem for self-publishers! The tools are legit helpful and the Black author focus is powerful. – **Beta Reader**

Your book is a mentor-in-print. It equips underrepresented writers with the tools and mindset to confidently share their stories. – **Beta Reader**

PERSONAL WELCOME FROM THE AUTHOR

Scan the QR code below to watch a short video where I share why I wrote this book, the mistakes I made, and how it can be your go-to resource on your publishing journey.

SCAN ME

OPEN YOUR CAMERA AND SCAN TO WATCH NOW

To every person of color who dares to share their stories with the world as a form of inspiration, liberation, and change.

May you do good work.

CONTENTS

Introduction
MY WRITING JOURNEY   **xiii**

PART ONE: CREATION
VISION AND WRITING

Chapter 1
THE REALITY OF WRITING A BOOK   **1**

Chapter 2
OWNING YOUR STORY   **9**

Chapter 3
DEFINING YOUR PURPOSE   **15**

Chapter 4
GATHERING YOUR IDEAS   **23**

PART TWO: POLISH
REFINEMENT & PREPARATION

Chapter 5
POLISHING YOUR MANUSCRIPT   **35**

Chapter 6
THE THREE READING PARTNERS   **49**

Chapter 7
FORMATTING FOR READABILITY   **61**

Chapter 8
THE STANDARDS OF FORMATTING   **71**

Chapter 9
THE WONDERFUL WORLD OF BOOK COVERS   **87**

Chapter 10
THE FINAL PREPARATION CHECKLIST   **101**

PART THREE: PRESENTATION
PRODUCTION & PUBLISHING

Chapter 11
DETERMINING WHERE TO PUBLISH   **111**

Chapter 12
THE SERVICE EXPERIENCE   **121**

Chapter 13
BOOK PRICING & PROFITABILITY   **137**

Chapter 14
PREPARING FOR LAUNCH   **143**

Chapter 15
THE VISIBILITY PLAN   **149**

PART FOUR: PROMOTION
LAUNCH AND MARKETING

Chapter 16
BUILDING YOUR LAUNCH TEAM   **169**

Chapter 17
AVOIDING MARKETING STRESS 183

Chapter 18
AFTER THE LAUNCH 195

Chapter 19
TURNING YOUR BOOK INTO A BUSINESS 201

Chapter 20
MODERN BOOK PUBLISHING TOOLS 209

Conclusion
YOUR STORY, YOUR RESPONSIBILITY 219

RESOURCES 223

ACKNOWLEDGMENTS 257

ABOUT THE AUTHOR 259

MY WRITING JOURNEY

HAVE YOU EVER hit that point where you said, "Forget it, I'll learn it myself"?

That was me a few years ago when I started my self-publishing journey. I was fed up with asking for help and getting nothing in return. It felt like everyone wanted to hold on to their secrets—secrets that could've saved me time, money, and more than a few cups of coffee. Instead, those secrets became my 3 a.m. caffeine-fueled lessons as I tried to figure everything out on my own.

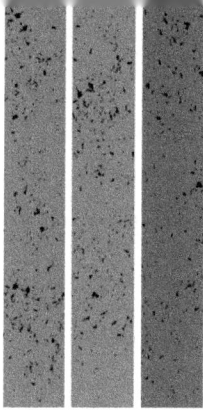

But the truth is, my writing journey began long before that moment. I didn't know I'd become an author or the steps I'd need to take. Life is like that sometimes, so you must figure it out.

You see, back in college, I wrote Facebook notes called "Mirror, Mirror," raw reflections and deep conversations with myself about life, healing, and the experiences that shaped me. Writing them felt liberating.

I printed those reflections, placed them in a binder, and moved on with life. But they awakened something in me, a creative side I didn't know I had. Years later, conversations with students, colleagues, family, and friends pushed me forward. People wanted to know how I faced the challenges I grew up with, how I dealt with pain, and how I kept moving forward.

I started writing chapters and saved them in a folder on the same laptop I'm using now. Then, like many writers, I stopped. Two years passed until one day, while driving home from work, something inside whispered, "Finish what you started."

That was the beginning of my real writing journey. But the truth is, I had no idea what I was doing. I reached out to someone who had published books, hoping for guidance, but nothing came of it. I had to take the long road of discovery, and it was a lot of work. I wasted more money than I want to admit and made mistakes. By my second and third publications, I figured out how to do this with excellence, without spending thousands of unnecessary dollars.

Now, many books later, both for myself and for others, I'm here to share what I've learned. And that's why this book exists.

WHY TELLING OUR STORY MATTERS

When I first became curious about representation in publishing, I asked myself: *Who actually gets published in America? And who decides which stories are told?*

The answers were sobering.

According to WordsRated's 2023 Author Demographics study, **81% of published authors in the United States are White**. Minorities make up only **19% of authors**, and within that, **5–7% are Black**.

The story doesn't get much better behind the scenes. The 2023 Lee & Low Diversity Baseline Survey revealed that **72.5% of those working in publishing identify as White**, while only **5.3% identify as Black or African American**. And those numbers have barely shifted in nearly a decade. This data appears again in the Resources section as a reference tool, but the bigger truth is this: it confirms why our voices, our stories, and our publishing choices matter more than ever.

Put simply, not only are fewer of us getting published, but even fewer of us are sitting at the decision-making tables in publishing houses. Lack of representation on both ends shapes which voices are heard, which stories are elevated, and which perspectives are too often overlooked.

This is why telling our story matters. Because when we publish, we do more than add another book to the shelf, we claim space in an industry that hasn't always made room for us. We inspire someone else to pick up the pen. We create a legacy that says: our stories belong here too.

As a Black-owned publishing company, I take this personally. My presence in this industry is proof that representation matters—not only in the stories being told, but in the people guiding and protecting them.

Self-publishing gives you that same power. You don't have to wait for approval from someone who may not see the value in your story. You have the autonomy to:

- Choose what to share.
- Choose how to tell it.
- Choose who your book is meant to help.

Ask yourself: *What if only one person reads my story, will it still be worth it? And what if the whole world reads it, am I ready for that level of transparency?*

The answer is, "Yes!" And, if you can sit with those questions and still feel the desire to write, then this book is for you and for us.

WHAT YOU'LL GET HERE

I need you to understand something up front: this book didn't come together overnight. It came from sacrifice, late nights, early mornings, money spent on things that didn't deliver, and mistakes that cost me both time and energy. I don't say that to impress you, but to show you I take your journey seriously.

At the same time, this book isn't meant to be an encyclopedia of everything ever written about publishing. That's not what you need, and it would only overwhelm you. What I've done here is strip away the noise to focus on the essentials, the lessons, the strategies, and the tools designed to move you forward.

Here's what you won't get:

- Fluff or hype.
- Unrealistic promises of overnight success.
- Disguised sales pitches for an expensive course.

Here's what you will get:

- Practical, step-by-step strategies.
- Templates, tools, and checklists.
- Honest insights on mistakes to avoid and tips for publishing with confidence.

I learned quickly that when you publish a book, you leave behind part of your legacy. You should be proud of it. I want you to produce a book as polished as something from a big-name publishing house.

WHO THIS BOOK IS FOR

In creating this book, I had to answer an important question: "Who are you writing this book for?" This is a question you'll need to ask yourself when self-publishing, because what you share, and what I share, isn't for everyone.

So, to answer my own question, this book is for nonfiction writers, especially aspiring authors from underrepresented backgrounds and cultures who lack abundant resources, who want to:

- Share their story through a memoir, leadership book, self-help guide, journal, or workbook.
- Publish with excellence without wasting money.
- Take control of their narrative and create a lasting impact.

Self-publishing requires effort, making it worthwhile. Expect late nights, long weekends, and doubts. If you're committed, this book offers the clarity, tools, and confidence to stay focused.

Don't worry, I'm not leaving you to figure this out alone. I'll walk alongside you with the information, charts, tables, templates, and insight packed into these pages. Think of this book as your publishing companion. I've got your back. Now, let's talk about how we're going to do it.

HOW WE'LL DO IT

When I started publishing, I didn't know where to start. Maybe that's where you're right now, or maybe you've tried before and felt stuck. Either way, I know how confusing self-publishing can feel. Over time, I discovered that when you follow certain steps in the right order, the process becomes clearer and the results much better.

I now use this simple framework to keep myself moving forward. It's also something I share with my clients during consultation meetings, so it's not something you can only get by working with me. And you're reading this book to learn how to do this yourself, right? I'm here to guide you and point you in the right direction.

In this book, we will follow what I call the **Four Phases of Writing & Publishing a Book**. In each phase, there are specific things you must, should, and could do. We'll explore each in enough detail to give you what you need to get started and move forward.

I will outline the must, should, and could do since flexibility matters. Depending on resources, you might do some extras to improve your position. But I emphasize this: our goal is for you to produce a high-quality product. What you publish reflects you.

With that in mind, let's begin with the first phase: Creation.

PHASE 1: CREATION (VISION & WRITING)

I believe every successful book begins with a clear vision. You are considering writing for a reason, and this phase is where you define your purpose, shape your message, and commit to the writing process.

As a self-publishing author, you control your production speed. However, many rush without clarity on their message, audience, or presentation quality. I've seen results that exceed simple grammar mistakes.

In this phase, clarifying your "why" keeps you focused when writing gets hard. Identifying your audience ensures your story reaches the right people. Outlining your chapters, organizing ideas, and building a writing rhythm help avoid writer's block and maintain momentum.

This phase isn't about perfection but authenticity and getting your story on paper. You'll revise multiple times. The words you craft form the foundation. Editing, design, and marketing can polish your work, but they can't replace the heart and clarity of strong, intentional writing.

PHASE 2: POLISH (REFINEMENT & PREPARATION)

This might be the most tedious phase of them all. I personally hated it. The back and forth of editing, reviewing different versions to be sure I captured my story, and letting others confirm if I met my intention was painful. But it was also liberating and worth it.

Once your draft is complete, the real transformation begins as you shape raw words into a professional book. Editing (developmental, copy, and proofreading) is essential. Self-publishing removes barriers but still requires meeting industry standards.

Beta and ARC readers are invaluable. They help gauge audience reception and refine key elements such as your bio, book description, and acknowledgments.

Administrative tasks like securing ISBNs, copyright, and Library of Congress Control Numbers establish ownership and professionalism. Skipping this makes your book seem unfinished, hurting credibility, while doing it well sets you up for marketplace success.

PHASE 3: PRESENTATION
(PRODUCTION & PUBLISHING)

This is where your manuscript becomes a real book. The production phase transforms your words into a polished product ready for the world to see. If you don't pay close attention here, you risk heavy scrutiny from reviewers. We'll go deeper into this later.

We'll cover interior formatting, which gives your book structure and makes it visually appealing and readable. A high-quality cover design attracts readers before they read a word. In self-publishing, presentation matters as much as content, so your book will sit alongside traditionally published works and should look professional.

Choosing the right publishing platforms, setting fair prices, and reviewing proof copies are crucial for your reach and reputation. Every detail, from spine text to how your eBook appears on devices, reflects your care. Rushing this stage can cause errors, poor experiences, or negative reviews.

When done excellently, this phase ensures your book meets industry standards and challenges the stereotype that self-published books lack the quality and detail of big publishers. Take this stage seriously, it's critical and may require extra time to perfect.

PHASE 4: PROMOTION

I'm reminded of the saying, *And knowing is half the battle*, in this phase. Why? Because writing and publishing your book is only half the process. There's a whole new world when it comes to promoting and getting it into the hands of readers.

This phase can be discouraging unless you can afford a marketing firm, which is unlikely since you're reading this. We'll explore strategies, tools, and how AI can support your launch.

The launch and marketing phase builds anticipation, engages readers, and establishes your presence as an author. A strong pre-launch plan with early reviewers and social media teasers creates buzz before your book hits the market. During launch week, promotion, email outreach, and community engagement can drive sales and reviews, providing a strong start. But marketing doesn't stop there.

Post-launch efforts like sharing testimonials, booking interviews, and joining book clubs or podcasts help maintain momentum. Many self-published authors underestimate this phase, hoping "the book will sell itself." But visibility takes effort. Your book will only sell if readers can see it.

Your book may carry life-changing messages, but without promotion, it risks being overlooked. A thoughtful marketing plan ensures your story reaches the people who need it most, turning your book from a personal accomplishment into a meaningful impact.

This book is packed with everything I've learned, the things I wish someone had told me when I started. I've included the checklists, strategies, and insights here, so you don't have to go searching for them. And if you ever reach a point where you'd like help walking through the process, that's why my company, **Keywords Unlocked**, exists, to come alongside authors like you.

Whether you do this completely on your own or decide to partner with us, you'll have what you need to begin right here in these pages.

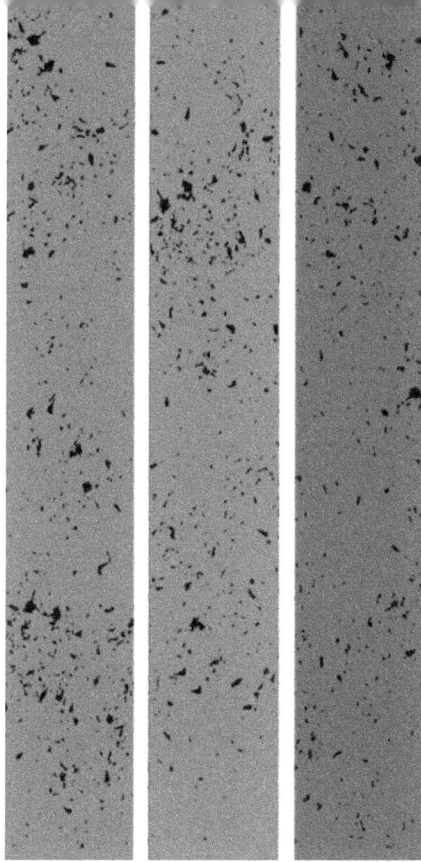

PART ONE: CREATION
VISION AND WRITING

CHAPTER 1

THE REALITY
OF WRITING A BOOK

BEFORE YOU WRITE A SINGLE WORD, let's have a real conversation. Writing a book, especially if you're self-publishing, isn't sitting at a desk with a cup of coffee, pouring out your heart, and magically ending up with a bestseller. It's a process that will test your time, patience, and discipline.

When I started my first book, I was full of motivation and divine inspiration. What I lacked was a roadmap. I didn't know the costs, the time it would take, or that finishing the manuscript was just the beginning. Another mountain awaited, called marketing.

And let me tell you this: I sacrificed a lot to get that first book written and published. But my reality may not be yours. I wasn't married, didn't have kids, and could close myself off from the world for weekends at a time to push through the book. You might be balancing family, a full-time job, or other responsibilities, which means your journey will look different. And that's okay. What matters is preparation. If you prepare for what's ahead, you'll already be miles ahead of most people who self-publish.

HOW IT STARTED FOR ME

When I first started writing, my routine lacked structure. No fancy desk. No high-tech equipment. No special pens or notebooks. It started with the Notes app on my phone. I'd type in the oddest places, during lunch breaks, late at night in bed, or on my drives to work. It wasn't unusual for me to grab my phone and use the voice recorder to capture my thoughts. I was laser-focused, tapping out what would eventually become multiple chapters of my book.

At that time, I had no idea what I was doing or knowledge of how to structure chapters. I did not know how long it would take or how expensive self-publishing could be. What I did know was this: I had a story to tell. It was enough to keep me moving.

If you're feeling the same way right now, excited, nervous, or even doubting whether you can do this, I get it. Writing a book, especially as a self-publishing author, can feel overwhelming at first. But as Nelson Mandela said, "It always seems impossible until it's done." And he was right. The key is to prepare yourself for the realities of this journey. It's a rewarding one you'll appreciate in the end.

As you prepare to start your writing journey, I want to share eight things I learned, with the hope that they will help you, too.

1. BE REALISTIC ABOUT THE TIME INVESTMENT

I need you to ask yourself right now: *Where is the time for this going to come from?*

Writing a book isn't something you squeeze into five spare minutes a week. It takes hours, writing, rereading, rewriting, and handling all the steps that come after. And those hours must come from somewhere.

When I work with clients, one of the first questions I ask in a consultation is, "How much time can you commit to this project each week?" I ask for two reasons. First, to understand how committed they are to finishing. Second, to get them to admit out loud that this is a commitment they must prioritize.

When I wrote, I sacrificed Netflix, weekends, and sometimes even sleep. Was it worth it? Absolutely. But it came with trade-offs.

Take a realistic look at your schedule. Can you dedicate 5–10 hours a week to writing? It might mean waking up earlier, staying up later, or giving up one or two weekends a month. If you can't find that time now, you'll need to either delay your project or adjust your expectations for how fast you'll finish. And that is okay, because I have had to do it myself. The point is to be honest about your capacity and set a realistic goal.

2. SET A PRELIMINARY BUDGET

Despite what you hear, self-publishing isn't free. Yes, you *can* technically write and upload a book for little to no money, but if you want it to look professional, it will cost you something.

Editing, cover design, formatting, and marketing all add up. You can save by doing some things yourself, but you should still plan for at least **$500–$2,500** if you want your book to compete with traditionally published titles.

For example, I have paid $100–$150 for cover design, $65 for copyright, $120 for ISBNs, $25–$50 per person for beta readers, and $75–$150 for formatting. There are still other costs, such as editing. Self-publishing is only free if everything is done alone. But in reality, only professionals can manage that successfully.

I wasted money in the beginning because I didn't know better. I paid for services without understanding what "good" looked like. I don't want that for you. Even with a small budget, plan now. Decide what you can invest upfront and what you may need to learn to do yourself.

3. RESEARCH THE SELF-PUBLISHING PROCESS EARLY

If you're holding this book, you're already ahead of the game. Most people don't think about the process until after they finish writing, and that's a mistake.

You need to understand what's coming before you get there. Writing is only one step. You also must edit, format, design a cover, upload your files, market your book, and manage distribution platforms like Amazon Kindle Direct Publishing (Amazon KDP) or IngramSpark.

I learned everything the hard way, staying up until sunrise, watching YouTube videos, and experimenting on my own. The smarter move is to learn now so you're not blindsided later.

4. EVALUATE YOUR PERSONAL NETWORK AND CONNECTIONS

You might be thinking, "Why should I think about people before I even write the book?"

Here's why: the people you know will play a big role in your book's success. They can become beta readers, advance reader copy (ARC) readers, or even help promote your book when it launches. But you need to start building those relationships now.

I recently spoke with a fellow author who was thrilled her book reached #1 on Amazon. I asked how she did it, and she said she spent 18 months building her network and connections through activities to generate excitement for her book. Remarkable. Most of us don't have 18 months to prepare, but if you do, I applaud you.

I did not think about this soon enough. I scrambled to find people who could help, and it cost me time. Learn from me. Do not make the same mistake. Build your network early through writing groups or people on social media.

5. UNDERSTAND WRITING IS ONLY HALF THE WORK

I'm going to say this plainly: **writing the book is the easy part**. If I knew then what I know now, my publishing journey would have been much smoother.

The other half of the process, the part most self-publishing authors don't prepare for, is marketing. Writing is about 20% of the process, while marketing often takes up the other 80% of the effort needed for success. If you want to sell your book beyond family and friends, you need to be ready to talk about it, post about it, and promote it long after you've typed "The End." This could mean creating fliers, hosting bookstore events, joining writing groups, speaking on podcasts, or even launching a book tour. It is work, but the goal is to make your book visible.

And let me add this as a bonus: **be okay with people getting tired of you talking and posting about it.**

This is why setting realistic expectations upfront matters. If you hate marketing, you'll either need to learn to embrace it or accept that your book may not reach a wide audience. And that's okay, if you know your goal.

6. PREPARE MENTALLY
FOR FEEDBACK AND CRITICISM

You're about to put your thoughts, your experiences, and your story out into the world. People will have opinions. Some will love it. Some won't.

This is a part of being an author. You need to prepare yourself now for the fact that beta readers, ARC readers, and reviewers will give you feedback that might sting. But you need those voices to make your book better.

I had to learn to swallow my pride and listen, even when I disagreed. Take the feedback, keep what helps, and let the rest go.

7. DECIDE ON YOUR PUBLISHING GOALS

What do you want this book to do for you? Do you want to sell thousands of copies? Establish yourself as an expert? Share your story for healing and legacy purposes? Your answer will shape your budget, your marketing efforts, and even how much time you invest.

For me, my first book wasn't about money, it was about telling my story. But for later books, I shifted my goals to include speaking opportunities and business growth. Be honest with yourself about why you're doing this. If you're not, you'll only end up frustrated when you don't get the results you claimed you didn't want.

When I wrote *Unshaken Leadership*, my goal was to advance my professional career. I did this by writing about my 30 years of leadership experience and positioning myself as an expert in the field. Yes, I was writing for leaders, but I also knew the potential it could unlock for me.

Now I'm in a position where I provide training, have my book included in leadership workshops and retreats, and speak on professional platforms. None of that would have been possible if I weren't honest with myself from the start. **You must be, too**.

8. COMMIT TO FINISHING

There will be moments when you want to quit. Every writer has them. I can't tell you how many times I almost gave up. Some days the writing felt too heavy, other days, I was simply tired of the process. But I kept going because I had already decided in my heart that I would finish.

I know you're serious about writing, because you're reading the last part of this first chapter. Well done. This tells me you have already made an important decision, a commitment to seeing this through. Keep going. Even if it takes longer than you planned, your story deserves to be finished.

CONCLUDING THOUGHTS

Writing and publishing a book is one of the most rewarding things you could ever do. It can also be one of the hardest. This is why I wanted to begin by giving you the truth about what it takes.

This book will guide you step by step or with adaptable strategies. You've already started by committing. Now, own your story and decide what to share with the world. Let's begin.

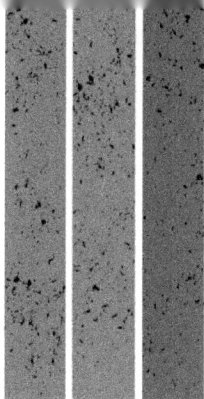

CHAPTER 2
OWNING YOUR STORY

TELLING YOUR STORY IS POWERFUL, but before thinking about publishing, you must ask yourself one important question: Why? It might sound simple, but your *why* will be the thing that grounds you when this process gets hard, and it *will* get hard.

Writing a book takes time, energy, and courage. There will be moments when you doubt yourself and moments when you want to quit. Your *why* will remind you why starting and finishing matter.

Stop for a moment. Grab a notebook or open your writing app and write this down: *Why do I want to write a book?*

Take your time answering. Be honest. Your answer might fall into one (or more) of these categories:

- **Legacy:** You want to leave something meaningful behind for your family or community.
- **Teaching & Helping Others:** You want to inspire, restore hope, or offer solutions to someone struggling.
- **Business or Professional Growth:** You want to position yourself as an expert in your field.
- **Personal Fulfillment:** It's been on your to-do list for years, and now you're ready to finish what you started.

Whatever your reason, own it. Because once you know your *why*, you can decide **who** you're writing for.

WHO ARE YOU WRITING FOR?

The second big question you need to answer is: **Who is this book for?** Then, follow up with, Who do you want to impact? Who will benefit from your story?

Think about the person you're writing to as if you're sitting across from them, having a conversation. Are they someone searching for hope? Does someone need practical steps to solve a problem? Do they need to feel less alone in their struggles?

Write down your answer in one sentence:

"My book is for _____ so that they can
_____."

For example: "My book is for first-generation college students so they can feel confident navigating higher education."

As a nonfiction author, especially if you're self-publishing, **you need clarity about your reader**. You are not writing for everyone. You are writing for the people who need your story the most.

MY JOURNEY TO OWNING MY VOICE

Earlier, I shared how I started writing in college. Those reflections were vulnerable and showed me evolving into the person I am today. In those pages, I was giving myself a voice.

But what I did not tell you is how it felt. Writing liberated me. I was talking to my innermost self, surfacing my thoughts, and finding solutions to problems I had been facing. It felt different. It felt like freedom.

For a little while on paper, I could be fully me. At that time, I was guarded. I lived inside a box. But when you own your voice in writing, the box breaks. Others begin to see themselves in your words. They feel free, too. For example, when I wrote my first book, I wasn't sure if I wanted to tell the world about the struggles I faced growing up. These included drug abuse, the lights being shut off, and the instability with my parents. When I embraced my voice, it unlocked opportunities for connection, and the outcome was life-changing.

This is where I want you to be as you write. Embrace your innermost self. That's where impact is made. That's how change begins. But it's hard to get there if you do not own your voice.

There's a self-publishing reality I want to share with you. It can be a lot, especially during this stage of writing. This is where being grounded in who you are and who you're writing to will support your goals in the end.

While there is flexibility in self-publishing, like when you decide to publish or what stories you tell, there are still logistical things you must keep at the forefront if you want to succeed. But the good news is you control your path.

Once I figured out the nuances, the sky became the limit. The only restrictions were the ones I placed on myself. The biggest one was holding myself accountable to quality. That's the power of self-publishing. Once you own your voice, no one else gets to decide what story you can or cannot tell.

OWNING YOUR VOICE AS A SELF-PUBLISHED AUTHOR

Aren't you glad no one gets to tell you what to write, how to write it, or whether your story is "good enough" to publish? Freedom is powerful. But it's not a reason to lower your guard when it comes to standards.

Traditional publishing houses often decide which stories are "marketable" based on business interests. If they don't think your story will sell, they reject it, not because it lacks value, but because it doesn't fit their sales goals. You get to change that in your publishing journey.

Self-publishing gives complete control. Write a memoir, a guide, a workbook, or even a book titled *Why I Believe the Sky Is Blue* if you want to. (*Will it sell? Maybe not. But the choice is yours*.)

This flexibility is vital for Black authors and other underrepresented voices. Too often, our stories are overlooked or reshaped to fit someone else's idea of what is acceptable. Self-publishing changes that by giving you the power.

But with that freedom comes responsibility. The reader must still be kept in mind. The story should aim to be transformational, insightful, or helpful. Owning a voice does not mean ignoring the audience, it means telling the truth in a way that resonates with them.

And here is something else: no one can tell your story better. It's the gift of nonfiction writing. Whether it's a memoir, a leadership book, or a self-help guide, a unique perspective is what will connect with readers.

A FINAL WORD BEFORE MOVING ON

Throughout this book, "Self-Publishing Advice" highlights are included. These are practical insights I learned the hard way. Use them along with the strategies, tools, and resources in these pages to position yourself to publish with confidence.

Remember, you won't change every life or sell thousands of copies overnight. But if a book helps even one person with hope, direction, or courage, that is success.

As we move forward, hold onto both the why and the story. By the time we finish, the path to publishing will be clear, and the story will be owned in a way that can change someone else's life.

CHAPTER 3
DEFINING YOUR PURPOSE

YOUR WHY WAS EXPLORED in Chapter 2, the reason for writing this book. Now, it's time to take that a step further and ask another critical question:

Who are you writing this book for?

You might think, "Well, I'm writing this for myself. It's my story." And to some extent, that's true, you may be writing to leave a legacy, to fulfill a personal goal, or to process your own experiences. But here's the truth:

Once your book is published, it's no longer about you.

There will be a real person on the other side of the pages. Someone reading the words and seeking something specific. The person might be looking for guidance, encouragement, a solution to a problem, or simply reassurance that they're not alone.

You have an important set of questions to ask yourself:

- **Who exactly am I writing to?**
- **What are they going through right now?**
- **What do they need from this book?**

The clearer the understanding of the reader, the stronger the writing will be.

DRILLING DOWN:
WHO IS YOUR IDEAL READER?

Let's get practical. Suppose you're writing a self-help book about building a computer program.

Who is it for?

- **Beginners** who've never coded before?
- **Intermediate learners** who know the basics but need advanced techniques?
- **Experts** who need insider strategies to scale their work?

It is impossible to write for all three at once. The audience shapes the writing, the examples chosen, and even the words selected.

And this is not only about writing. It is about marketing, too. The way a book is positioned, from its title to its category on Amazon, depends on knowing the intended reader. If this is not figured out early, the wrong people may buy the book, feel it was not meant for them, and leave negative reviews. Not because the book is bad, but because it was not written for them.

Think of your book as a product. It's designed for a specific type of person, to solve a particular problem, in a certain way. Who is that person to you?

Understanding an audience goes beyond demographics or surface-level traits. It is about clarity of intention. Is the writing for them, offering guidance, encouragement, or solutions? Or is it to them, speaking directly into their experiences as if sitting across the table? Distinction matters because the way a message is framed shapes how it's received.

FOR VS. TO:
UNDERSTANDING THE DIFFERENCE

Earlier, we discussed your why. Now, we need to define who, and that involves understanding the difference between writing for someone and writing to someone.

The "for" statement is about purpose, why you're writing and who you hope to inspire in a general sense.

The "to" statement is about precision, exactly who the writing addresses and what that audience needs.

Here's the difference side by side:

PURPOSE (FOR)	TARGETED READER (TO)
My book is for aspiring writers who don't know how to get started with the writing process.	My book is to Black aspiring writers between the ages of 25–55 who want to publish a book without compromising their personal story.
My book is for single mothers who want to rebuild their lives after divorce.	My book is to single mothers, ages 30–45, working full-time, who need practical steps to manage their finances and heal emotionally after divorce.
My book is for college students who feel overwhelmed by life after graduation.	My book is to first-generation college graduates, ages 22–27, who are struggling to transition from college to their first job.

See how the "to" statement forces specificity? It transforms a book from a general encouragement into a targeted tool. As you write, tools like this will prepare you for various stages of authorship. From defining your why, to answering questions about who you wrote for, to shaping marketing materials. It all serves a purpose. But why is this important? There are three key points I want to highlight to help clarify the question.

WHY IS THIS IMPORTANT?

Why does this distinction matter so much?

1. **Writing becomes sharper:** When the exact reader is pictured, the words feel personal, like a conversation with a friend, not a lecture to a crowd.
2. **Marketing becomes easier:** Clarity about the audience makes it simpler to choose a title, subtitle, categories, and even the type of social media posts to create.
3. **Readers feel seen:** A book that speaks directly to them is the one they recommend, review, and remember.

WHAT I LEARNED THE HARD WAY

Let me share a mistake I made early in my writing journey. I believed I knew my audience, young Black boys in tough environments who needed hope beyond societal labels. The problem was that my title didn't clearly communicate that.

My first book was originally titled and published as *Oakland Hills, Milwaukee Rivers*, and that was all. No subtitle. No explanation. If you saw that book sitting on a table, you might have thought it was about geography or travel, not a personal story of survival, identity, and purpose.

Later, I came to understand the importance of subtitles and realized how much I had limited my reach. Adding a clear, descriptive subtitle helped the right readers find it.

Why does this matter? Because without identifying the reader early, time can be wasted, sales can be lost, and the chance to reach those who most need the message may be missed.

STEPS TO DEFINE YOUR READER

It is time to put this into action and move forward on the self-publishing journey. Writers may be at different stages in the process. Some have already completed a manuscript, which is expected. Even so, this exercise is valuable to confirm that all requirements of the publishing process have been met.

STEP 1: WRITE YOUR PURPOSE STATEMENT (FOR)

This keeps you grounded in *why* you're writing.

My book is for _____ **so they can** _____.

Example: *My book is for single mothers rebuilding their lives after divorce so they can regain confidence and create financial stability.*

STEP 2: IDENTIFY YOUR TARGET AUDIENCE (TO)

This guides you further and helps you clearly visualize who you're talking to.

My book is to _____ **who** _____ **so that** _____.

Example: *My book is to Black aspiring writers between the ages of 25–55 who want to learn the ins and outs of publishing a book without compromising their personal story so that they can avoid mistakes.*

STEP 3: ASK YOURSELF THESE QUESTIONS

To improve your "TO" statement even more, answer the following:

- *What problem does my book solve for them?*
- *What do they want to feel after reading this?*
- *What kind of transformation do I want them to go through?*

You might be wondering, *Why are these questions important?* Good question.

The reason is simple: at some point, readers will be asked to buy the book. When that moment arrives, they need a reason, a compelling incentive, to say yes.

People buy books to solve a problem. Every book addresses a problem, regardless of the genre. For instance, someone reading a suspense novel isn't only looking for entertainment, they're solving the problem of boredom. They're escaping their daily routine and immersing themselves in something exciting and unpredictable. If you want your book to be considered good, it needs to do the same thing.

STEP 4: PICTURE YOUR IDEAL READER

Give the reader a name, an age, and a personality. Imagine sitting across from that person, having a conversation. When writing, direct the words to them.

When I wrote my first book, I pictured a 10-year-old boy sitting on a dusty carpeted floor, watching a 12-inch black-and-white TV, trying to navigate life while uncertain about the future. Writing became a way to understand and share what he was thinking, the challenges he faced. It also helped me explore what might have happened if he had not escaped, and what I hoped readers would take from his story to reflect on their own.

For you, aim to be as detailed.

Example: *I'm writing to Monica, a 32-year-old single mom who's working full-time and scrolling through this book at 10 p.m., hoping for practical advice that feels doable in her busy life.*

Doing this now will prevent headaches later, especially in marketing. A clear title, subtitle, category, and even social media posts will feel more focused when the intended reader is defined.

CHAPTER TAKEAWAYS

The person who picks up a book may never meet its author, yet they are inviting that voice into their life for a reason. They are searching for something, and a story can be what changes their outlook, shifts their mindset, or gives them hope.

As you prepare to gather your ideas, keep that reader in mind. Writing is not only about sharing words on a page, but also about creating impact that reaches straight to the heart, the struggles, and the hopes of another person.

CHAPTER 4

GATHERING YOUR IDEAS

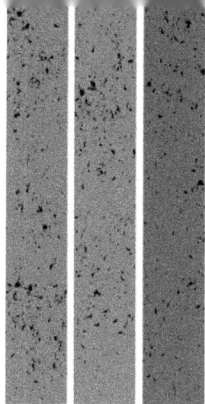

BY NOW, YOU UNDERSTAND WHY this book matters and who it's meant to reach. Clarity puts you ahead of most people who sit down to write. The next challenge is turning intention into structure. Many new authors make the mistake of diving straight into writing, hoping the pieces will come together later. That approach often leads to frustration, wasted time, and unfinished drafts. Gathering your ideas first changes everything.

Let me save you some frustration upfront. It will not happen instantly. When I first started, I had no idea where to begin, so I created a process. It began with gathering ideas and mapping out the lessons or stories I wanted to share. A dry-erase board became the tool for drafting an outline of what to cover. From there, the thoughts were organized and the chapters arranged to make sure they connected. My outline became the framework. But why is a framework necessary?

WHY YOU NEED A FRAMEWORK BEFORE YOU START WRITING

Writing without direction makes chapters feel scattered, with unclear messages, and leads to wasted time rewriting. A book should feel deliberate, and a strong framework helps achieve that.

Think of your book as a road trip. The destination is already known (the why and the reader), but now it needs a GPS, a clear path that leads there without unnecessary detours.

As we move through this chapter, several exercises will be provided to guide the process. Remember, this is not a step-by-step manual but a resource to help move toward publishing a book. Still, the information will be valuable. Grab a pen or pencil and some paper, because they will be needed for the exercises.

These exercises are also available in "Gathering Your Ideas" within the Resources section, so there is no need to write in this book, unless you want to, since you did buy it.

CHOOSING THE RIGHT TYPE OF NONFICTION BOOK

Before outlining, it's important to understand what kind of book is being written. Not every nonfiction book is the same, and that was a lesson learned through experience. After researching book genres, I gathered the information shared below.

The four primary nonfiction book types:

1. **Memoir / Personal Story:** Shares life experiences to motivate, connect, or provide perspective.
2. **Self-Help / Motivational:** Emphasizes solving a problem or inspiring change.
3. **How-To / Guidebook:** Explains a process, framework, or set of skills.
4. **Workbooks and Journals:** Interactive tools for reflection, exercises, and personal development.

You might be wondering, "Can they be combined?" Absolutely. My first book is mainly a memoir, but it also weaves in motivational undertones through personal quotes and offers advice and perspectives readers can learn from. This book serves as a guide while incorporating my story to keep it relatable. Writers have the same flexibility to blend approaches.

EXERCISE 1: WHAT TYPE OF BOOK ARE YOU WRITING?

Write down which category your book primarily falls into and why – if it's a blend, note which one is your *focus*.

_____

_____

_____

_____

ESTABLISHING THE CORE MESSAGE & PROMISE OF YOUR BOOK

Once you identify your type, you should define the main promise of your book.

Ask yourself:

- *What's the main transformation I should see in my reader after they finish?*
- *What's the main point I want them to remember, feel, or believe?*

Use this simple template:

By the end of this book, the reader will _____.

Examples:

- *By the end of this book, the reader will know exactly how to self-publish a professional-quality book without wasting thousands of dollars.*

- *By the end of this book, the reader will feel hopeful about healing from childhood trauma and will have practical steps to start that journey.*

This statement will guide every chapter you write. If a section doesn't support that promise, it doesn't belong in the book.

EXERCISE 2: WRITE YOUR CORE PROMISE

Fill in the blank:

By the end of this book, the reader will _____

_____

_____

_____

_____

_____

BRAIN DUMPING YOUR IDEAS (FREE WRITING & MIND-MAPPING)

Now that the book type and promise are clear, it's time to get every idea out of your head. One way I do this is through a process called a **brain dump**. This powerful technique helps clear the mind and uncover hidden connections between ideas.

But here's the key: **don't worry about order, grammar, or polish yet.** The goal is to get it *all* out first.

You can do this in three ways:

1. **Free Writing:** Set a timer for 20 minutes and write nonstop about anything related to the book, stories, lessons, memories, quotes, statistics, or even questions to explore. Let the thoughts flow freely without judgment.

2. **Mind-Mapping:** Start with the book's main idea in the center of a page. Branch out to related themes, moments, and subtopics. This visual layout reveals natural groupings and connections between ideas.

3. **Voice Notes:** If talking feels more natural than typing, record freely about the ideas. This is especially helpful for processing complex thoughts or unlocking passion that may not surface through writing.

In two of my publications, mind-mapping was used to identify major life moments, followed by free writing scenes connected to each. This process helped uncover raw emotions and details that might have been overlooked otherwise.

A brain dump, which you'll do in the next exercise, serves as the first creative release. It silences the inner critic and creates space for clarity.

Once everything is on the page, patterns begin to emerge, and from those patterns come structure and strategy. Do not skip this step. It is where the book truly begins.

EXERCISE 3: BRAIN DUMP SESSION

Set a timer for 20 minutes and write everything that comes to mind about your book. Don't stop to edit, dump it all out.

_____

_____

_____

_____

_____

_____

_____

_____

GROUPING IDEAS INTO THEMES (THEMED BUCKETS)

Once your ideas are out, it's time to sort them into categories (themes). Identify natural patterns:

- Memoir writers should group their stories by life stages or major events.
- Self-help writers group by steps, strategies, or principles.
- Guidebooks are arranged by process stages or skill levels.

For example, this book uses Four Phases (Creation, Polish, Presentation, and Promotion), a clear, bucketed framework that helps you follow along step by step.

EXERCISE 4: CREATE YOUR BUCKETS

Review your brain dump and organize ideas into 3 to 7 main categories. Write them down, these will probably become your chapters or sections.

1. _____

2. _____

3. _____

4. _____

5. _____

6. _____

7. _____

CREATING YOUR OUTLINE (YOUR BOOK'S ROADMAP)

Once your buckets are ready, you can start building your outline.

At its most basic, every nonfiction book follows a three-part structure:

1. **Introduction:** Explain why this topic is important and why the reader should trust your expertise.
2. **Main Content:** The essential chapters where you teach, share, or inspire.
3. **Conclusion:** A final summary, call to action, or reflection.

For each individual chapter, follow this simple formula:

Story or Example → Lesson or Insight → Practical Step or Reflection for the Reader.

An outline does not need to be perfect. Think of it as a roadmap, not a restriction. It can always be adjusted along the way.

EXERCISE 5: DRAFT A SIMPLE OUTLINE

Write your chapter titles (or working titles) based on your buckets. Under each one, list 2–3 key points or stories you want to include.

_____

_____

_____

_____

_____

_____

_____

_____

_____

_____

_____

_____

_____

SETTING REALISTIC WRITING GOALS & DEADLINES

Outlines give direction, but deadlines provide momentum.

Here's what you need to decide:

- **Word Count Goal:** Most nonfiction books range between 30,000 and 50,000 words.
- **Weekly Writing Goal:** 1, 500–3,000 words per week is realistic for most beginners.
- **Deadline:** Choose a target date for finishing your first draft.

EXERCISE 6: SET YOUR WRITING GOALS

Target word count: _____

Weekly writing goal: _____

First draft completion date: _____

ENCOURAGEMENT & REALITY CHECK

We have covered a lot, and it may feel overwhelming. But look at what has already been accomplished. Ideas, memories, lessons, and messages have been captured straight from the heart. This is the beginning of something powerful, and it's worth celebrating. Congratulations, be proud of this moment.

As promised, doing the work, staying committed, and giving time leads to progress, and it has already begun. The next step is where it gets exciting: shaping what has been created into something sharp, clear, and purposeful. Do not worry about perfection yet. This stage is about refinement, turning raw words into something lasting and professional.

Keep the why and the reader in mind. Every revision and decision helps build a book that could be a breakthrough. The foundation is laid. Now it's time to refine it into something remarkable with each word, edit, and bold choice.

Welcome to Part Two: Polish.

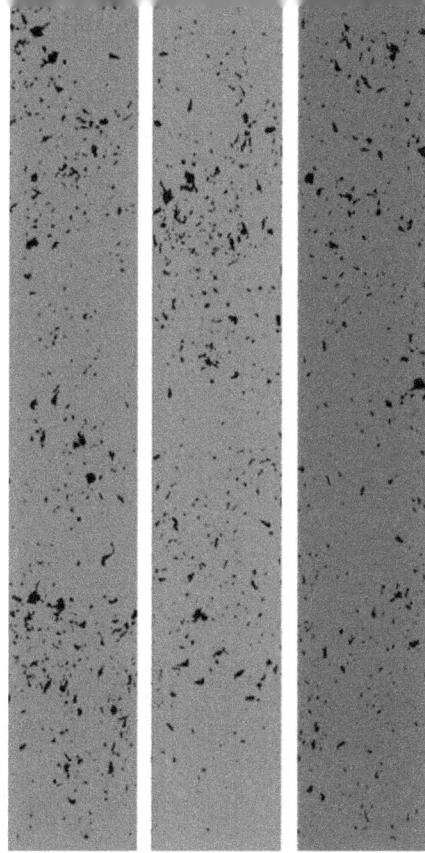

PART TWO: POLISH

REFINEMENT
& PREPARATION

CHAPTER 5
POLISHING YOUR MANUSCRIPT

DO YOU KNOW WHAT A MANUSCRIPT IS? This is a question I should have defined from the start, because understanding it's key to professionalism. It is a term every aspiring author needs to know.

This is more than an essay. A manuscript is a carefully crafted, intentional collection of your work, the result of time, effort, and focus, that will eventually become a book. It must meet industry standards if you want to be taken seriously.

People spend countless hours, months, or even years fine-tuning manuscripts to achieve quality. In my opinion, every manuscript must be reviewed carefully to ensure it's held in high regard.

And since this book is in your hands, I will assume the goal is to be better than those who throw words together and call it a book, right? Let us dive deeper into what polishing a manuscript takes.

WHY POLISHING MATTERS

Let me share a quick story with you. I once wrote a book and was so excited to share it with the world that I rushed through the editing process. I thought, "It is my story. People will feel my heart. That's enough."

It wasn't.

I didn't think my book was trash thrown together. But deep down, I knew I could have spent more time, time that would have left no room for anyone to question my professionalism.

When time is invested in a book, it shows respect to the audience, the exact people spending money to support it. Think about it: you would not walk into a store and buy a dirty pair of jeans, right? The same standard applies to a book. If readers are expected to pay for your book, make sure it's clean, polished, and worth every dollar.

How would I know? Because I quickly learned readers do not only read for heart. They read for clarity, flow, and professionalism. Typos and awkward sentences pull them out of the message. A story that could inspire suddenly feels amateur because of something as small as a misplaced comma.

Here is me owning my truth. One of the reasons I wrote this book is because I saw too many of my people putting out books that were less than professional and thinking it was okay. It is not.

For Black authors, there's an additional, unfair layer of scrutiny. Whether we like it or not, we're often expected to prove we are as good, if not better, than our White counterparts. This means we can't afford to cut corners. We must take the time to learn, refine, and produce work that reflects excellence.

Quality takes time, but it's worth it. Family and friends may support you no matter what, but strangers will not hesitate to leave brutal reviews, and trust me, those reviews will humble you fast.

This is why polishing matters. A name, a reputation, and our collective credibility as Black authors depend on proving to the world that we can produce high-quality, professional work.

These standards are universal for all authors, but I feel it's important to highlight them for my people. You are part of my purpose. Helping us show up with excellence in this space is one of the reasons I wrote this book.

Self-publishing does not mean sloppy publishing. A book carries a name and a brand. If readers are expected to trust the work, it must look and read as professionally as anything from a big publishing house.

FIRST DRAFT REALITY CHECK

Here is the first thing to accept: the first draft is supposed to be messy. Every great book begins as a rough draft. No one writes a perfect first draft, so be kind to yourself.

When I first started writing, I edited as I went. I would write a paragraph, dislike it, delete it, rewrite it, and delete it again. Hours passed, and only three sentences sat on the page. Do not be too hard on yourself. Writing and editing are two separate stages. The only task in a first draft is to get the story out of the mind and onto the page. Refinement into something beautiful comes later, during the polishing phase.

Think of a first draft as clay. Clay may be messy, but it's exactly what is needed to shape something great later.

You may have already begun this process. But if not, how do you move from having an idea to creating a manuscript?

When I started my rough draft, I used my cell phone. Yes, my cell phone, and my most prized possession, the Notes app.

I added my outline and began writing. For months, I typed whenever I had free time. On a trip to Tennessee with friends around Halloween, I sat in the passenger seat typing as ideas came. I already knew the story I wanted to tell and the moments to emphasize, so I jotted them down. Some of those notes later became full chapters.

Later, I discovered another trick: voice recording my thoughts and organizing them afterward. This saved me so much time, especially when preparing a resource on recording an audiobook. I learned that technique from a guy on YouTube, and it completely changed how I approached getting my ideas out quickly. You may also find this strategy helpful.

The draft stage is about getting ideas out of the head and onto paper. Whether typing, writing by hand, or recording voice notes, the goal is simply to get the words down. Polishing comes later.

THE THREE LEVELS OF EDITING

Professional-quality books go through three editing stages. Even if you self-edit most of it, you should understand how these levels function.

1. DEVELOPMENTAL EDITING (THE BIG PICTURE)

This emphasizes the structure and flow of a book and asks the writer to consider a series of questions that will help position the manuscript for success.

These questions help guide the developmental process:

- "Does the book make sense throughout from start to finish?"
- "Are the chapters arranged correctly?"
- "Does each chapter connect to your book's promise?"
- "Is there a smooth flow or transition between chapters?"
- "Are there gaps where a reader could feel confused?"

When writing, consider a few key aspects. In a memoir, are the life events arranged to create a clear emotional journey? In a how-to guide, are the steps in the right order? If not, take time to make sure the book delivers a strong reader experience.

Let me share a problem I faced when writing my first memoir. I had so many stories to recall that I nearly lost track of the timeline. I spent days working on each chapter, printing them out and spreading them across a table like puzzle pieces to arrange them in order.

It was nerve-wracking. There was a moment when I almost gave up, thinking it was not worth it. But what kept me going was knowing that if the timeline was off, readers could be completely confused, especially with my frequent trips back and forth to California.

Because of that, I made it my responsibility not to release anything below my standards. As I shared earlier, Black authors often have to work harder in this industry. That was one way I held myself accountable to that standard.

I challenge you to do the same. Stay committed to quality, but be realistic about what can and cannot be done. Progress, not perfection, is what keeps you moving forward. Just never compromise on putting out your best work.

Now let us shift into some practical tips and strategies to make this process easier, and ways to save money along the way.

Developmental editing can range from $500 to $2,500 depending on length and complexity. Yet much of it can be managed by the author through careful outlining, beta reader feedback, and dedicated time.

For example, developmental editing often takes a simple draft and strengthens it for clarity and impact:

Original draft:

My first semester in college was rough, but I made it through.

Edited version:

My first semester in college nearly broke me. Between two jobs, endless homework, and the loneliness of being away from home, I often wondered if I would make it. Finishing that semester taught me the resilience I still carry today.

This is what developmental editing does. It goes beyond grammar to sharpen structure, emotion, and flow so the writing connects with readers.

When feedback came in from my beta readers, it gave me a chance to decide whether to update the work or keep it as it was. In some cases, especially with the second edition, I carefully considered their input and made adjustments. At other times, I chose to keep what I had written because changing it would have compromised my original intent.

Either way, the process is crucial. **Beta readers are not there to boost confidence. They help ensure the standards set for the book are maintained.** Even if every suggestion is not used, reviewing feedback carefully guarantees that what is published is intentional and professional.

2. LINE EDITING / COPYEDITING (THE SENTENCE LEVEL)

This is where the book's readability is refined.

- **Are the sentences clear and engaging?**
- **Are words repeated or filler phrases overused?**
- **Is the tone consistent throughout the book?**

For nonfiction, this step helps the writer sound like the authority they want to be. A polished, confident tone builds reader trust.

When I worked through this step, I used Artificial Intelligence to spot overused words. I uploaded my manuscript into ChatGPT and used this prompt: "Write like an expert book proofreader and determine overused words that would negatively impact the reading experience." This single step helped me identify words to replace.

Example: One of my overused words was *really*. ChatGPT flagged it as unnecessary in several places.

Original draft: *It was really hard to stay focused on writing.*

Edited version: *It was hard to stay focused on writing.*

A simple change, repeated dozens of times, made a big difference in readability.

I also exported the manuscript to a PDF and read it aloud, listening for repeated words. When I noticed one, I used Ctrl + F to search the entire file. If it appeared too often, I replaced it with a more precise alternative.

Did this take time? Absolutely. But it was worth it for a better reading experience. This is the kind of investment a self-publisher must be willing to make.

There is always the option to hire a professional for this work. Expect to pay around **$0.02–$0.05 per word for professional copyediting**. If the budget is tight, complete a thorough self-edit first. The cleaner the manuscript you hand over, the less time (and money) you will spend on professional services.

3. PROOFREADING (THE FINAL POLISH)

This is the last step before you hit publish. Proofreading catches:

- Typos and punctuation errors.

- Inconsistent formatting (chapter titles, page numbers, spacing).
- Misspelled names, incorrect facts, or missing references.

Example of Proofreading:

Uncorrected draft: "Inauthentic leadership are one of the most damaging forces in any organization."

Corrected version: "Inauthentic leadership is one of the most damaging forces in any organization."

A small slip in grammar like this may seem minor, but it instantly affects readability and credibility. Proofreading catches those details before readers do.

Never skip this step. Seriously, never. Skipping it is the equivalent of a Black woman walking into the mall without her wig while her hair is still in three-week-old braids.

It is that serious. You do not want that kind of attention, the kind that jeopardizes integrity and professionalism. A single typo on the first page can make readers doubt everything else you wrote.

I assume that, going forward, you will review what I write with a fine-tooth comb, looking for any editing mistakes. **As you should.** No worries. This is my pet peeve, and I take it seriously because every word is an extension of who I am.

Bring the same level of pride to your work. Do not sabotage your impact by saying, "This is good enough," and skipping the hard work of double or even triple checking the manuscript.

When I researched how to self-publish, I repeatedly came across reviews from readers who were disappointed with poorly formatted books. Many had negative things to say, not about the story itself, but about how distracting the errors were.

I even had a personal experience with this. I supported a friend who wrote a book and found a major error: a repeated section in one of the chapters. The book wasn't self-published; it had been released through a publisher. As much as I wanted to focus on the story, I couldn't get past that mistake. It immediately lowered my perception of the book's quality.

You do not want readers telling stories like that about your work. It is not worth it. Do the work upfront so you can sleep at night knowing your book reflects the standard you want to be known for.

SELF-EDITING STRATEGIES BEFORE HIRING HELP

A lot can be done before paying for an editor. Here is the system I use to save both money and time:

- **Read Aloud:** Read the entire manuscript out loud. If you stumble over a sentence, readers will too.
- **Print It Out:** Seeing the work on paper tricks the brain into reading it like a reader instead of a writer.
- **Use Editing Tools (Cautiously):** Grammarly, ChatGPT, or ProWritingAid can help with grammar. Do not rely on them for tone or flow. You do not want tools to change your authenticity, so pay close attention. (More on this later.)
- **Reverse Outline:** Create an outline from what has already been written. If chapters feel out of order, rearrange them now.
- **Take a Break:** Step away for at least 3–5 days, then return with fresh eyes. If possible, extend the break to 30 days for a complete reset.

Use the "Self-Editing Prep Checklist" in the Resources section of this guide. Print it and physically check off each step before moving on to professional editing. This extra layer of diligence will save time, money, and unnecessary frustration later.

WHEN (AND WHO) TO HIRE

You don't need to hire everyone at once. But you *do* need to know when to bring in help.

I believe you're ready to hire when you experience one of these moments in your review process:

- You've self-edited to the best of your ability.
- You've had at least 2–3 beta readers review your draft.
- You can't see what's wrong anymore because you've read it too many times.

If you decide to hire an editor**, do your due diligence in choosing the right one**. I've heard horror stories of people paying for services only to find out later that the person they hired didn't have the skills to complete the job.

This even happened to me, not with editing, but with a cover design. I wasted over $100 because the designer couldn't produce the quality I needed. I had asked for samples of their work, but looking back, I'm not sure the samples were theirs.

Like my cover design experience, you want to protect yourself from situations like this.

Here are some tips to help you choose the right editor:

- **Ask for a sample edit:** Most editors will edit 1–2 pages for free or at a minimal cost, so you can evaluate their skills.
- **Ask for recommendations:** If possible, request a reference from a previous customer. If they have public reviews, reach out to one of those reviewers for honest insight.

- **Get a contract, and never pay full upfront:** A reputable editor should be established enough to begin the work with partial payment.
- **Find someone experienced with your genre:** For memoirs, self-help, or guidebooks, make sure the editor has worked on similar projects before.

Self-Publishing Advice: Websites like Fiverr.com can be helpful because they host many freelance editors who specialize in different types of books. However, carefully check their reviews, look at their previous work, and verify their credibility before hiring.

FORMATTING CONSIDERATIONS AT THIS STAGE

Formatting comes later, but it's important to start thinking about design now. Editing decisions made at this stage will affect the final layout.

When I first went through this process, I reviewed every book in my house, studying formatting, spacing, and design. I wanted a clear idea of what I hoped to accomplish with my book's interior. As a creative, I did not want my book to look exactly like others, but there were elements I appreciated. These features reflected quality and contributed to a positive reading experience.

When you cross over into becoming both an author and a publisher, your eyes change. You stop looking at books only for their stories and start noticing how they're built.

Here is my recommendation: start paying attention now. Pick up books you enjoy and study what you like and do not like, margins, spacing, headings, fonts, and even how paragraphs are broken up. By the time you're ready to format your final manuscript, you will approach that stage with a clear vision of the outcome you want.

In the process, ask yourself:

- *Do you want callout boxes, charts, or exercises?*
- *Are there sections that need bullet points or spacing for clarity?*
- *Are your chapter titles consistent in length and style?*

Make these decisions now to avoid revision headaches later. When you hand files to the formatter, unclear choices slow the process and extend the turnaround time. Every choice should be deliberate and aligned with your vision for the book.

ENCOURAGEMENT & REALITY CHECK

This phase takes patience. By now, you have poured your heart into the words. Polishing can feel slow and tedious. Do not lose sight of the bigger picture: the book will live beyond you. Every page reflects your name, your brand, and, for us as Black authors, your credibility.

My friend, take your time and do it right. When someone picks up your book and sees how clean, clear, and professional it is, they will respect the work and trust you. Trust becomes the foundation for something far greater than sales.

The next chapter focuses on relationship. This is where the people you're connected with come into play. As you begin gathering feedback through beta readers and ARC readers, you're inviting others into your creative process.

These readers are your first audience. Their reactions, questions, and insights reveal what resonates and what needs refinement. More importantly, they mark the beginning of a relationship between you and the people your book is meant to serve.

Writing is personal. Publishing is public. But between the two is a sacred space where connection happens. Listen to your readers. Honor their feedback. And let their engagement sharpen your message so it lands exactly where it needs to.

You're not only writing a book; you're developing a writing reputation. One that speaks on your behalf long after you've written the final word.

Before you move forward, pause and ask yourself:

What do you want your book to say?

Who do you want it to reach?

The clearer you're about these answers, the more focused your writing will become. With that clarity, you will be ready to take the next step: transforming your ideas into a manuscript that you can refine, polish, and proudly share with the world.

CHAPTER 6
THE THREE
READING PARTNERS

BUILDING ON THE IDEA OF YOUR LEGACY from the last chapter, let's now talk about how others can help you refine and enhance the experience your future readers will have.

Before pressing the "publish" button, make sure the manuscript has been reviewed by more than one set of eyes. Yes, this is your project and your story. But it's also written for an audience that expects something excellent.

The strategy of using **beta readers, ARC readers, and sensitivity readers** can elevate a manuscript from good to great. While **highly recommended** as an industry best practice, using these readers isn't technically required, though it's certainly something you *should* do.

Why? Because it can come with a cost. Having someone perform these services for you takes time, and for many people, **time is money**. Rightfully so, you should respect and honor that.

If this practice is implemented, it's wise to compensate those who take on any of these roles, even if they volunteer their time. Paying them shows respect for their effort and acknowledges the contribution they make toward producing and enhancing the quality of your book.

In this chapter, you'll learn not only what beta readers, ARC readers, and sensitivity readers do, but also how to find them, manage them, and gather their feedback in a way that genuinely improves your book. I'll guide you through the practical side of the process, from recruiting readers to setting expectations, to collecting and analyzing their input, so you can confidently decide what to incorporate and what to leave out. By the end, you'll understand how to turn reader feedback into a useful tool, not a hurdle, on your publishing journey.

BETA READERS: YOUR FIRST LINE OF DEFENSE

Beta readers are your secret weapon for early feedback, and this is often the most valuable in your writing process. I learned about beta readers when writing my first book, but I misunderstood their purpose. I mistakenly used them as if they were **ARC readers**, focusing on early reviews instead of constructive feedback.

Why? Because I was sensitive about letting anyone read my work, but also ignorant. I chose the self-publishing route specifically because I didn't want anyone controlling what I wrote, so the idea of handing my draft over to strangers felt uncomfortable. **Bad mistake.**

While I learned from my mistake over time, I eventually realized that beta readers aren't there to control your story—they're your partners. They provide an unbiased opinion and help you see how the world will receive your book, which is important during your writing process. This is part of your developmental process, which I'll discuss later in this book, to help you write and tell your story better. My advice as we enter the next section is to find people you don't know.

BETA READERS VS. ARC READERS

You might be wondering, "What's the difference between a beta reader and an ARC reader?" Great question, and it's one you need answered when self-publishing.

- **A beta reader** gives you feedback during the draft stage. Their job is to answer this primary question: "If I bought this book for myself, how would I feel about what you (the author) wrote?" They help identify what works, what doesn't, and where readers might get lost.
- **An ARC reader** reads your polished, fully edited manuscript before it's released. Their goal isn't to change anything, it's to provide an honest review so others know how your book impacted them.

In short, **beta readers provide feedback to YOU; ARC readers give feedback to the WORLD.**

Both are valuable, but don't confuse the two like I did. Use them at the right stage, and your book will be stronger for it.

HOW MANY BETA READERS SHOULD YOU HAVE?

This is a valid question, and the answer is, it depends. It takes time to collect feedback, analyze it, and turn it into usable themes that can improve your writing. Below are some recommendations to get you started:

Choose 3–5 beta readers who:

- Are in your target audience.
- Will give honest, constructive criticism.
- Are not close family or friends who simply want to be nice.

When working with beta readers, give them **specific instructions so that their feedback is valuable**. I've provided a "Beta reader & ARC reader" tool in the Resources section, but here's a quick exercise to guide you now:

Ask your beta readers to answer questions like these:

1. What was most helpful or inspiring?
2. What felt confusing or unclear?
3. Did anything feel repetitive or unnecessary?
4. Would you recommend this book to someone else? Why or why not?

Organize their feedback in a spreadsheet and look for patterns. If three or more people mention the same thing, pay attention and consider making adjustments to improve the reader experience.

Their job is to provide constructive feedback; **your job is to decide where and how to integrate it without losing your voice or intention.**

A LESSON FROM MY OWN EXPERIENCE

If I had the advice I'm sharing with you now, it would have saved me months of revisions and frustration on my debut memoir. After releasing it, I started receiving feedback that was helpful, but would have been much more useful before publication. During my process, one beta reader pointed out that I had mistakenly titled the book *Oakland Hills, Wisconsin Rivers*. Even though I had read the manuscript a million times, I had missed it. Another beta reader noted that one of my chapters didn't provide enough depth regarding a character, which helped me better understand the reader's perspective. Collectively, that feedback prompted me to revise and release a second edition, because I wanted to create a stronger experience for readers.

How would you feel if you received online reviews that said, "Your book doesn't read well," "This book has poor grammar," "You should stop writing," or even, "I want my money back?" Do this step early to save time, money, frustration, and disappointment.

ARC READERS: YOUR PRE-LAUNCH ADVOCATES

As shared before, ARC readers have a different responsibility in the writing process, and they are directly tied to how the world will perceive your book once it's published. You want reviews when you go live, and part of their job is to provide them.

Choose 7–10 ARC readers who:

- Are in your target audience.
- Understand the nature of your project.
- You can trust with your manuscript.
- Are not close family and friends.
- Can commit to your publishing timeline.
- Will provide the needed review when your book is released.

Think of ARC readers as preliminary book ambassadors. Their role is to help future readers know why your book matters, not to help you rewrite it. Treat them with the same level of professionalism as paying customers, because their reviews will influence how others perceive your book.

In my experience, identifying ARC readers (30–45 days before your book launch) is a reasonable timeframe. However, you need to build a buffer into your schedule because, even when people say yes, life happens.

If you're four weeks from your release, set a deadline of at least two weeks for others to read your manuscript. When I revised the Second Edition of my memoir, I used this strategy. Of the seven ARC readers I recruited and sent my manuscript to, three didn't finish.

However, the four who did, provided strong, detailed feedback that helped me gauge how well the book would resonate with readers based on my goals.

One excellent strategy I used, and recommend, is providing ARC readers with a 30-question feedback document to complete. The insights they shared were not only valuable for my revisions but later became a powerful marketing tool. I quoted them in a "What Advance Readers Are Saying" section to add credibility to the book's impact.

For transparency, I compensated each ARC reader $125.00 and gave them a free copy of the book after it was published. I later learned that was *very* generous and not what I would recommend to you. A lesson learned as ARC readers *shouldn't* be paid money.

The benefit was that many of them went on to become advocates for the book, posting about it on social media and vouching for its impact. It helped to earn me additional book sales and visibility, a small, but impactful contribution.

SENSITIVITY READERS: PROTECTING ACCURACY AND AUTHENTICITY

If your book deals with cultural, racial, religious, or other sensitive topics, consider hiring a sensitivity reader.

For Black authors especially, this is critical when writing for a broad audience. You want to ensure that your message is understood as intended and not misinterpreted or unintentionally offensive. Sensitivity readers help catch blind spots you may not even realize exist.

What is a Sensitivity Reader?

A sensitivity reader is a professional who reviews your manuscript for cultural accuracy, respectful representation, and authenticity. For example:

- When writing about a culture that is not your own, sensitivity readers can help confirm whether the portrayal is accurate.
- When sharing experiences related to trauma, identity, or marginalized groups, sensitivity readers help ensure harmful stereotypes are not unintentionally reinforced.

Sensitivity readers can be found through professional networks such as Reedsy, editorial collectives, writing groups, or by reaching out directly to communities represented in the book. Their role is not to censor the writer but to help maintain credibility and integrity, especially within the communities the work seeks to reach.

Now that you know who these readers are and why they matter, let's move into the next step: gathering and managing their feedback. The process I'm about to share works for beta readers, ARC readers, and sensitivity readers alike, and it will help you collect the kind of insights that strengthen your book.

GATHERING AND MANAGING READER FEEDBACK

It's one thing to know what beta, advance, and sensitivity readers are, it's another to manage the process of gathering their feedback.

This step can feel overwhelming if you don't have a plan in place, but once you set up a system, it becomes smooth and repeatable.

When I recruited beta readers for one of my projects, I started in Facebook groups designed for authors and readers. I shared a short post with the book title, total word count, and compensation (for example, $1.00 per 1, 000 words). Instead of handling replies in the comments, I asked anyone interested to send me an email. This extra step cut down on bots and made sure only serious readers followed through.

From there, I created two Google Forms (you can use any survey tool or even paper if that works for you).

- **Form One: Participation Confirmation**. This form gathered their first name, last initial, email, and confirmed they understood the expectations: timeline, payment after completion, and what they were committing to. At the end of this form, I embedded a link to the PDF manuscript and a second Google Form with my evaluation questions.
- **Form Two: Feedback Collection**. This form contained all the questions I wanted readers to answer after finishing the manuscript. In the Resources section of this book, I've included sample questions you can adapt for your own use.

The same system works for ARC readers and even for sensitivity readers, with only small adjustments to the questions you ask.

Once feedback started coming in, I downloaded the responses and looked for recurring themes: where readers were most engaged, where they were confused, and any areas that felt weak. The goal wasn't to change everything someone suggested but to identify patterns that pointed to strengths and areas for improvement.

BALANCING FEEDBACK WITH INTENT

Gathering feedback is only half the process, knowing how to use it is where the real growth happens. You invited beta readers, ARC readers, and sensitivity readers into your journey for a reason. They invested their time and energy into your work, and that input deserves to be taken seriously. Feedback, when approached with the right mindset, can transform a good book into a great one by helping you see blind spots you might otherwise miss.

It's also why I believe it's often better to include readers you don't know personally. Friends and family may mean well, but their feedback can be clouded by bias. A stranger has no reason to sugarcoat their response, which often makes their perspective more valuable.

As you review what comes in, take the time to look for patterns. One offhand comment doesn't necessarily mean you need to change something, but when multiple readers point out the same issue, a confusing section, a weak transition, a chapter that drags, that's a signal worth paying attention to. Consistency often reveals truth. Lean in and listen to your readers, they're showing you how to refine the experience.

At the same time, remember this: feedback is guidance, not a command. You must balance what you hear with your intention as the author. When I worked on the Second Edition of my memoir, I sometimes made changes based on feedback to improve clarity and flow. But I also kept certain passages untouched to preserve their original meaning. The balance every author must strike is listening without losing your voice.

Use feedback wisely. Don't take it personally. You're the author, and the final decision is always yours.

COMPENSATING YOUR READERS

At the beginning of this chapter, I talked about "The Readers," as I'll call them in this section, being people with competing priorities and real-life obligations. Because of that, I believe it's only fair to compensate them for their contribution.

But what's considered reasonable?

There is no set rule for compensating people who support you in this way. However, you should always give them something as a way of saying thank you. Whatever you decide, be reasonable based on the time they are investing, reading your book in the evenings, on weekends, or after a long day at work. And if your book does exceptionally well, maybe even hits a bestseller list, you don't want them to feel like their valuable contribution wasn't appreciated.

Think of them as **partners** in this process, almost like temporary employees. Appreciate their time, insight, and opinions because they're helping you make your book stronger.

I've compiled some reasonable recommendations to help you accomplish this task. You can adjust these suggestions, but remember: these are people you've built relationships with, do right by them.

RECOMMENDED COMPENSATION AND APPRECIATION IDEAS

There's no one right way to thank readers. Some prefer payment, others appreciate recognition, free books, or small gestures. Choose a method that fits your budget, matches the feedback level, and feels genuine. Below are options for compensating and appreciating beta, ARC, and sensitivity readers.

For Monetary Compensation: While not every author chooses to pay readers, offering monetary compensation is a practical way to acknowledge the time and effort they invest in your manuscript.

Beta readers:

- $25–$75 depending on the length of the manuscript and the depth of the requested feedback.
- Consider providing a gift card if cash feels too transactional.

ARC readers:

- ARC readers should *not* be paid for reviews or public feedback. However, you can show appreciation in ethical ways—such as providing a free advance copy, early access to materials, or including them in your acknowledgments.
- If you want compensated early feedback, that's considered a **beta reading service**, not an ARC review.

Sensitivity Readers:

- $100–$500 depending on their expertise, length of manuscript, and complexity of the cultural/sensitivity review.
- Professionals often charge per word ($0.01–$0.03) or per hour ($30–$75/hour), so clarify expectations upfront.

For Non-Monetary Compensation: If direct payment isn't possible, or if you'd like to add something more personal, there are plenty of non-monetary ways to show appreciation that still make your readers feel valued.

- **Free Copies of the Finished Book**: Signed, with a personalized thank-you note.
- **Name Recognition:** A "Special Thanks" section in the acknowledgments listing their contribution.
- **Early Access to Future Projects**: Offer them the chance to be part of your next book journey.

- **Social Media Shoutouts**: Publicly thank them and tag them (if they're comfortable with that).
- **Gift Cards or Care Packages**: $10–$25 cards for coffee, Amazon, or bookstores go a long way.

CONCLUSION: EXCELLENCE THROUGH COLLABORATION

Self-publishing gives you autonomy, but not isolation. The best books are shaped with others who help you see what you can't and strengthen your work before it reaches the world.

Beta, ARC, and sensitivity readers are part of your team. Value their time and insight, and use their feedback to sharpen, not control, your voice.

Now you know how to find these readers, manage their feedback, and use it to make your book stronger. Most of all, you've learned how to turn feedback into a tool that positions you to publish with confidence and excellence.

CHAPTER 7

FORMATTING FOR READABILITY

AFTER YOUR MANUSCRIPT IS WRITTEN and polished to the best of your ability, the next important step is formatting.

What exactly is formatting? Simply put, it's arranging your words on the page so that they look and function like a professional book, whether that's for a printed book or an eBook. This includes setting margins, choosing readable fonts, spacing paragraphs correctly, adding page numbers, creating consistent chapter headings, and making sure nothing looks out of place.

A well-formatted book guides the reader's eye smoothly across the page. A poorly formatted one distracts them with uneven spacing, awkward breaks, or text disappearing into the gutter (that inner margin where the pages meet). Formatting is the bridge between your manuscript and a finished, professional-looking book.

WHY FORMATTING MATTERS BEFORE YOU HIT PUBLISH

You may be thinking, "Does formatting matter if my story is good?" The answer is: **Absolutely.**

Readers notice bad formatting, sometimes more than they notice your actual story. Uneven spacing, inconsistent chapter headings, or text that runs too close to the margins will instantly make your book feel amateurish. And here's the harsh truth: a sloppy-looking book can make people question your professionalism, no matter how powerful your words are.

Think of formatting like the packaging on a product. You could have the best story in the world, but if the presentation looks cheap or rushed, readers will doubt its quality.

Formatting isn't about being "fancy." It's giving your readers the best possible experience to focus on your story and not your mistakes.

Here's why you can't treat formatting as an afterthought:

- **First impressions are everything:** A clean, professional interior signals to readers (and reviewers) that you care about quality.
- **It affects readability:** Poor spacing, bad line breaks, or tiny font sizes can make readers put your book down, even if the content is amazing.
- **Reviews will call it out:** I've seen reviews that said, "Great content, but hard to read because of the formatting." You don't want that on your name.
- **It represents your brand:** Like I said in earlier chapters, your book will outlive you. The way it looks will influence how people talk about you as an author.

Formatting is like wearing a suit to an interview. The suit doesn't change your skills, but it changes how people *perceive* them.

MY HARD LESSON ABOUT FORMATTING

During one of my projects, I thought I was almost done. I had written the story, edited it to death, and polished it until I couldn't see straight. I had watched what felt like millions of YouTube videos, read countless articles, and downloaded templates from every corner of the internet.

But it quickly became overwhelming, and I realized I needed help. Not because I couldn't eventually figure it out, but because it would take too much time, and I didn't have the patience. There is nothing more frustrating than trying to add headers, footers, and page numbers to your manuscript, only for everything to shift out of place no matter what you do. Even worse, you follow a YouTube tutorial only to discover it's outdated and no longer matches the current version of Word. Your screen looks nothing like what they're showing.

This was the beginning of what I learned about formatting, and why it's one of the most critical steps in producing a high-quality book.

At one point, I thought I could format my eBook for free using Draft2Digital's (D2D) platform. It has a built-in tool that lets you upload your Word document, and in theory, it should format your book automatically. But here's what they don't tell you: your document must be set up a certain way, or the system will produce something that looks nothing like a professionally formatted book.

When I uploaded my manuscript, my excitement turned into a nightmare. The margins were off, the spacing felt awkward, and the text was inconsistent, too small in some places, too cramped in others. It didn't "look" like a real book. I was devastated and frustrated all at the same time.

My friend, self-publishing will test your patience. It's why I eventually sought help, and even then, the process wasn't perfect. I share this not to discourage you, but to prepare you for the reality of doing this yourself. Formatting requires time, skill, and a lot of patience, whether you DIY or hire someone.

THE MOMENT I REALIZED I NEEDED HELP

After enduring endless frustrations, I turned to Fiverr.com and underwent a careful vetting process. I checked reviews (he had a solid 4.8-star rating) and studied his portfolio of previous work. His examples looked great, so I hired him. But here's another reality check: no one tells you about the back-and-forth required to get the final product the way you envision it.

Remember earlier when I told you to study other books and pay attention to formatting? This is exactly why. Even with a professional formatter, I had a specific vision for how I wanted my book to look, and I wasn't satisfied until it matched that vision.

When I finally received my formatted manuscript back, it was better than what I submitted, but it still wasn't perfect. There were issues, uneven spacing, misaligned words, and small inconsistencies. It took several rounds of revisions to get it right.

Part of the problem was on me: I submitted a manuscript that wasn't thoroughly proofread. Because it wasn't ready, I kept making edits, which caused more delays. Let me say this to you now: before you reach this step, ensure your manuscript is truly ready.

Because I outsourced this job, every round of revisions came with a turnaround time of at least three days. And each time I received the file back, I had to review the entire manuscript to ensure everything was correct. Sometimes, when one issue was fixed, another would appear elsewhere. By the end, the relationship between my formatter and me had grown personal, we went back and forth so many times that we were practically co-authors.

Here's something else you should know: I was formatting both an eBook and a paperback at the same time. These are two completely different formats, and what works for one doesn't automatically work for the other. Each requires its own careful adjustments to achieve a professional final product.

I can't stress this enough: formatting is about creating an experience, not merely making a book look pretty. When a book is formatted correctly, readers focus on your story and your message. When it's not, they notice every awkward paragraph break, every crooked line, and every word that gets swallowed up in the gutter (that inner margin where the pages meet).

As self-publishing authors, and especially as Black authors, we often don't receive the benefit of the doubt. People are quick to criticize, so we must hold ourselves to the same standard as traditionally published books, if not higher.

LESSONS LEARNED: FORMATTING THE RIGHT WAY

I uploaded my manuscript and sent it to the formatter with some apprehension. *Did I make all the intended changes?* I wondered. The honest answer: No.

That lingering thought sat with me for a few hours until I finally gave in and made a few last-minute edits. Then I reached out, hoping they could still be incorporated.

"This isn't formatting anymore, this is editing," he replied. "I'd normally have to charge you more for that."

My heart sank. I had already spent more than I'd budgeted for this project.

But then, a few minutes later, he messaged again: "However, this time, I'll do it for free."

I was relieved.

I share this moment because the courtesy my formatter extended isn't guaranteed. As authors, we must take the time to thoroughly prepare our work before passing it on to the next stage of the publishing process.

Below are some lessons I learned the hard way.

1. **Don't rush into formatting:** Submit your manuscript only when it's final, proofread, polished, and ready. Every edit after formatting costs you time and frustration.
2. **Expect back-and-forth, even with professionals:** Formatting is rarely perfect the first time. Be patient and prepared for multiple revisions.
3. **Treat eBooks and paperbacks as two separate projects:** What works for one won't automatically work for the other. Each requires its own careful attention.
4. **Professionalism matters more than you think:** Sloppy formatting makes readers doubt everything else you wrote, even if your content is great.
5. **As Black authors, we must hold ourselves to a higher standard:** We don't always get the grace for mistakes, so aim for excellence that rivals traditionally published books.

WHEN TO CONSIDER DIY FORMATTING

You have two options: do it yourself or hire someone. Both are valid, but be honest about your skill level and the amount of time you have available.

That was the crossroads I faced with this book. I decided to handle all the formatting myself, and it took me weeks to complete it properly. From reviewing the rules and double-checking spacing to ensuring consistency and aligning everything with industry standards, it was a big sacrifice.

If you decide to do this yourself, make sure you're up for the challenge. But know it's a rewarding experience to realize you did something remarkable with your own hands.

However, what are the things you should consider when facing the decision to format your book yourself or hire a professional?

Professional formatting can cost anywhere from $100 to $500, depending on the complexity and the length of your book. And trust me, it's worth every penny if you can afford it.

If you decide to take the DIY formatting route, don't worry. The next chapter provides a comprehensive tutorial on industry standards. The insight I share has been invaluable for me and has served as a reference time and again, even as I wrote this book and designed "how-to" guides for my website, because this can be a cumbersome task. I encourage you to be patient during the process because it's tedious and requires a strong sense of detail.

Below is a chart to use for DIY or outsourcing formatting. You might find it useful for your initial decisions.

DIY Formatting	Outsource Formatting
You're on a strict budget.	You want a polished, industry-standard look with minimal stress.
You're willing to spend hours learning software like **Microsoft Word**, **Vellum** (Mac only), **Atticus**, or **Adobe InDesign**.	You're short on time and need it done right the first time.
You have the patience to test, adjust, and proofread multiple times before finalizing.	You're writing a book with complex layouts (like workbooks, journals, or books with charts and graphics).

FORMATTING DIFFERENT FORMATS: PRINT VS EBOOK

Print and digital books require different formatting approaches:

- **Print Books:** Pay attention to margins, page size (most nonfiction uses 6x9 inches), and print-safe fonts.
- **eBooks:** Use simple formatting. Too many design elements can break when readers change font size or read on different devices.

If you're releasing both formats, you'll need two separate files: one for print and one for digital.

YOUR FORMATTING PREP EXERCISE

Because formatting is time-consuming and can vary from book to book, here's what I recommend doing before formatting yourself or hiring someone:

1. **Look at five books you love in your genre:** Pay attention to how the chapters look, how wide the margins are, and how the text flows.
2. **Write down what you like and don't like:** Do you prefer wide spacing? Do you want decorative chapter headers or clean, minimalist designs?
3. **Decide your trim size:** For most nonfiction books, **6x9 inches** is standard, but check what others in your niche are using.
4. **Budget for formatting now:** Even if you're DIYing, you may still need to pay for software or templates.

FINAL THOUGHT

Formatting may not feel creative or exciting, but it's as important as the words you write. A poorly formatted book screams "amateur," no matter how great your content is.

And remember: the world can be cruel, so invest in quality. We don't always get grace for mistakes, so we must meet, and exceed, industry standards. It's not pressure; but an opportunity to show our stories and voices belong in the same spaces as traditionally published bestsellers.

Take the time to do this right. Because when your reader picks up your book, you want them focused on your message, **not your margins**.

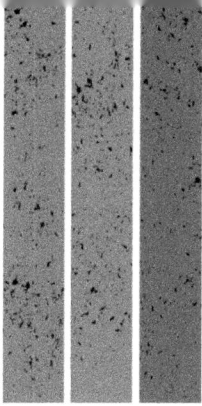

CHAPTER 8

THE STANDARDS OF FORMATTING

WRITING A BOOK is like inviting someone into your home.

Think about it, you've spent weeks, months, maybe even years telling people why they should "visit." You've talked about how important this book is, how it's going to change lives, or how it's the story they've been waiting for. This is your why, the invitation that convinced them to show up.

Now imagine this: they finally pull up to your house. Before they even step inside, they form an impression. "Oh, this is nice. I can't wait to see more," or "Hmm... this doesn't look like somewhere I want to stay long." That's your cover and back cover, their first judgment of your work before they even open it.

They walk up to your front door. Is it sturdy, well-framed, and inviting, with clean glass and a polished handle? Or is it shaky, with chipped paint and a rusty lock? That's your title page and copyright page, the details that quietly communicate professionalism or carelessness.

You open the door, and they step in. Immediately, they glance around at your interior, your light fixtures, your furniture, the art hanging on your walls. That's your dedication, preface, prologue, and introduction. These are the first moments they spend with you, deciding whether they feel comfortable enough to stay.

You invite them to sit down. They settle into your couch, and in that moment, they decide whether it's strong, supportive, and worth sitting on for a while, or whether it feels cheap, like it might collapse under them. That's your chapters, the heart of your home, where real conversation happens. If the experience here isn't good, they won't stay long.

Toward the end of the visit, curiosity gets the best of them, and they wander toward your backyard. Does it live up to the beauty of the rest of the house, or is it neglected and overgrown? That's your acknowledgments, references, notes, and index pages, details most people don't talk about but still notice if they're sloppy.

Finally, they thank you for inviting them over. They step out the door, smiling, and maybe say, "I'll be back" or "I'm telling my friends about this place." That's your About the Author page, their final impression of you, the person behind the book.

All this matters. Every page, heading, and spacing choice is part of the experience you're giving your reader. Much like a guest leaving your home, readers will walk away from your book with a lasting impression of both your story and you. Make sure it's a good one.

In the rest of this chapter, we will explore the details of what formatting involves based on industry standards and the specifics of what is recommended based on research and best practices.

UPHOLDING STANDARDS

We all have standards, and publishing is no different. When I sat down to decide what needed to be included in this book, this topic was at the top of my list. As self-publishing authors, many of us simply don't know the rules, what to use, when to use it, and how it should look, and that ignorance can sabotage our credibility. And let's be real: in my competitive nature, we need to be as good as, if not better than, traditionally published authors. As the young folks say, "Sorry, not sorry."

I am sure you notice that this chapter isn't a 200-page formatting manual. You're not going to get every technical detail here. What you're going to get are the essential tools and insights you need to start thinking like a professional. This is the kind of knowledge that will immediately set you apart if you're starting your writing journey.

Is this chapter important? Absolutely. People do judge a book by its cover, and its layout. You can have the most powerful story in the world, but if your book looks like you slapped it together in Microsoft Word over a weekend, readers won't take you seriously. And that, my friend, is a problem.

As self-publishing authors, especially as Black authors, we don't always get the benefit of the doubt. Traditional publishers have set the bar high, and whether we like it or not, we must meet or exceed it. The way your book looks is part of your message.

This chapter will break down the major parts of a book's structure and the formatting standards you need to know. Once you understand these basics, you can decide what works best for your book, and make those decisions with confidence.

Let's talk about each one, real, simple, and in plain English.

FRONT MATTER & STRUCTURAL ELEMENTS

TITLE PAGES: HALF AND FULL

The **Title Page** is the first page of the book. There are two types: half title and full title. It always begins on the right-hand side of the manuscript.

The half-page should only feature your book's title. Why do I say only? Because if you have a subtitle, industry standards suggest not including it. For example, if your full book title is "How to Sell 1000 Books: A Guide to Marketing," the half page should only display "How to Sell 1000 Books." That was a lesson I learned, and this was even when I hired a formatter. They did it wrong, too!

The full title page includes the book's title, subtitle, author name, and, if applicable, the publisher's name or logo. It appears later in the book, right before the copyright page.

For many readers, the title page is your first professional handshake, the moment that leaves a lasting impression. It should always be used, even in journals and workbooks, to maintain professionalism. The recommendation is to keep your title page clean and, if possible, visually consistent with your book cover. This small detail tells the reader you respect their experience.

When paying a book cover designer, ask them to give you an image of your title design to use inside your book. Doing this small step adds thoughtfulness to the reader. What if they refuse? Don't worry, you can also use AI tools like ChatGPT to recreate it in standard black for this purpose. The title pages in this book were created that way. Truth moment: I did it for this book!

When I formatted my first book, I almost skipped making this page look polished because I thought, *Who cares? They came for the story*. Wrong. It sets the tone for everything else.

As you continue to write, start paying closer attention to title pages in other books. Notice the uniformity and professionalism, it's an easy way to understand what's standard in the industry. It will also help you to recognize when companies are creative in how they style their books overall.

Here's a simple example of a clean title page:

Half Page Example:

HOW TO SELL A MILLION BOOKS

Full Page Example:

HOW TO SELL A MILLION BOOKS

A Guide to Marketing

Keyimani Alford

Keywords Unlocked Publishers (Logo)

COPYRIGHT PAGE

The Copyright page is a required page in every book. This is the page with the legal language that protects your work. The text you include here isn't fluff, it's how you officially claim ownership of your content, so you must always use it.

Later in the book, I'll go into more detail about the copyright registration process, which you'll want to review. But for now, know that the copyright page is used in every book format, eBook, paperback, hardcover, and even audiobooks. Maintaining this standard is a crucial part of your self-publishing journey.

Self-Publishing Advice: If you're publishing through **IngramSpark** or **Amazon KDP**, make sure the copyright page lists your ISBN and publisher name **exactly** as they appear in their system. Even a small typo can cause delays in approval.

Example:

DEDICATION PAGE

The **Dedication** page is a personal way to honor someone special. It's usually one or two sentences, but can be longer if you choose. Many authors use it to recognize someone who influenced their journey, giving readers a glimpse of their heart. Dedications are most common in memoirs, inspirational works, or books tied to personal experiences.

For my first book, I dedicated it to young boys and girls who felt life had forgotten them, because that was my "why." You may have a similar homage, and if you do, use it. It's a small page with a big emotional impact. While most are one or two sentences, I've also seen them stretch into a couple of paragraphs. Whatever you decide, make sure it's meaningful.

Example: For Aunt Grace, who taught me resilience by the water's edge.

ACKNOWLEDGMENTS

The Acknowledgments page is your chance to thank the people who supported you throughout your writing journey. It can appear either in the front matter (at the beginning) or the back matter (at the end) of the book, there's no strict rule.

This page builds goodwill, especially with those who directly contributed to your success, such as editors, beta readers, mentors, or even family members who encouraged you along the way. You should include it if others played a role in helping you bring your book to life.

If you truly did this alone or want to maintain a clean, minimalist design, it's fine to skip it. Just make sure if you do, that it's meaningful. According to industry research, "75% of nonfiction readers read the acknowledgments page" in books, primarily because it's personal. This is why it should be meaningful.

Self-Publishing Advice: Keep your acknowledgments short, 1–2 pages at most. Readers don't want to wade through 10 pages of thank-yous. Be sincere, be specific, but keep it concise.

THE INVITATION TO YOUR BOOK

In the beginning, I had no idea what the differences were between a Preface, an Introduction, or an Author's Note. Honestly, I thought they were "cool" to have because I saw them in other books. But as I grew as a writer, I learned there's a science, and a purpose, to when and why you use them.

These opening elements shape the reader's first impression and frame the way your message is received. Used well, they can build trust, establish credibility, and set the emotional tone for everything that follows. This next section will help you understand how these pieces work so you can decide which ones fit your book best.

PREFACE

A Preface is your personal note to the reader explaining why you wrote the book. It's designed to build a connection with your audience before they dive into the main content. You should use a Preface when there's a deeper significance behind your book, when the "why" matters as much as the "what."

For example, if you lost someone close to you and, through your grieving process, discovered strategies to help others heal, you could write a Preface to share that journey. It sets the tone and creates trust with your readers.

Example Opening:

"This book was born out of late nights at my desk, not because I wanted to be an author, but because my community deserved the truth about self-publishing, raw and unfiltered."

AUTHOR'S NOTE (NOTE FROM THE AUTHOR)

An **Author's Note** is your direct conversation with the reader. Unlike a Preface, which focuses on *why* you wrote the book, an Author's Note can include personal reflections, disclaimers, or additional context that helps the reader understand the content better. It's often written in a more casual, personal tone, as if you're sitting across the table with them.

You should use an Author's Note if:

- Your book discusses sensitive or potentially triggering topics, and you want to give readers a heads-up.
- You need to clarify creative choices, historical context, or research methods.
- You want to share a personal connection to the content, but didn't include it in the main narrative.

You don't need to include an Author's Note in every book, but it can be powerful when you want to set expectations for the reader or deepen their understanding of your intentions.

Example Opening:

"Before you dive into these pages, I want to say this: This isn't just a publishing book; it's about reclaiming our stories and telling them with excellence. If you're holding this book in your hands, know that every word was written with you in mind."

Self-Publishing Advice: If you include both a Preface and an Author's Note, keep them distinct. The Preface explains *why* you wrote the book, while the Author's Note speaks directly to the reader about *how* to approach it or what you want them to know before (or after) reading.

PROLOGUE

A **Prologue** is optional and is typically used to tell a story, set a scene, or create an emotional hook before the main content begins. It works exceptionally well in memoirs or narrative nonfiction where you need to pull the reader in emotionally right away.

I used a Prologue in one of my books because I wanted to immerse readers in the emotional core of the book before gradually building to the main story. It turned out to be one of the best writing decisions I made.

When to skip it? If you're writing a step-by-step guide, a Prologue may feel unnecessary and can slow down the reader's momentum.

INTRODUCTION

The Introduction tells the reader why this book matters and acts as your pitch. If done well, it convinces them to keep reading. Every nonfiction book should include an Introduction, even practical guides.

Example Template:

"By the end of this book, you'll understand exactly how to publish a professional-quality book without wasting thousands of dollars."

EPILOGUE

An **Epilogue** is an optional, reflective closing that gives readers a sense of "what happened after" or offers a final thought. It's perfect for memoirs or personal stories where readers want closure or an update.

I think of the Epilogue as the "after the credits" scene in a movie, it leaves readers reflecting and sometimes hints at what's to come. It's also a great tool if you're planning to release future content or a follow-up book.

CONCLUSION

The **Conclusion** is your final wrap-up, summarizing the key points and leaving readers motivated, inspired, or ready to take action. Unlike the Epilogue, which is optional, a Conclusion is **non-negotiable** in nonfiction.

Think of it as your last opportunity to speak directly to your reader, where you pull together the threads of your message, remind them why they picked up your book in the first place, and point them toward what comes next. A strong Conclusion doesn't simply restate the chapters, it reframes the journey and reinforces the transformation you've been guiding them toward. Done well, it ensures your book ends with impact rather than a fizzle, leaving your words echoing long after the final page is turned.

ABOUT THE AUTHOR

The **About the Author** section is your professional bio and acts as your mini-resume. It builds credibility and markets you for future opportunities like speaking, coaching, or consulting. Always include this section, regardless of your book type.

And please, use a professional headshot. A clean, high-quality photo helps readers connect with you as a real person and reinforces your professionalism as an author.

INTERIOR DESIGN & LAYOUT STANDARDS

The content in this next section helps ground us in one of the most important parts of publishing, readability.

Have you ever picked up a book where the font sizes were inconsistent, the spacing felt off, and the entire thing looked like a kid running wild on a playground? Just absolute chaos. This is precisely how your book will feel to readers if there's no uniformity throughout your manuscript.

I watched countless YouTubers advising about fonts, sizes, margins, and more in the beginning, trying to figure this out. Some of that advice was solid, yes, you shouldn't have 20 different fonts or random text sizes, but I found out a lot of it comes down to personal choice.

The key is to remember this: there are industry standards that readers subconsciously expect when they pick up a professionally published book. Even when I've outsourced formatting, I've spoken up whenever something looked off. Every decision, from the size of your headings to the spacing between your paragraphs, affects how comfortable and enjoyable the reading experience is. And as a self-publishing author, you owe your readers that level of care.

FONTS & SIZES

The font you choose is the first silent communicator of professionalism in your book. Before a reader even dives into your words, the typeface sets the tone. A clean, readable font tells them you care about their experience, a poorly chosen one screams amateur hour.

For printed books, serif fonts like Garamond, Georgia, or Times New Roman, sized between 11 and 12 points, are considered the industry standard because they are easier on the eyes and flow naturally across the page. On the other hand, sans-serif fonts like Arial may work for eBooks but often look cheap and unpolished in print.

Your genre also influences your choice. **Inspirational, self-help, and business books benefit from classic fonts** because they convey authority and credibility. **Children's books or creative works can get away with more playful fonts**, but even then, readability should always take priority.

I encourage you to think about your font as much as you think about your words; it shapes how your message is received.

SPACING & PARAGRAPHS

Spacing and paragraphs are the rhythm of your book. Get it wrong, and it instantly feels off. Readers may not consciously notice good spacing, but they will notice bad spacing.

The **standard for print books is a line spacing of 1.15 to 1.5**, which gives the eyes enough room to breathe without feeling stretched. In most cases, **each paragraph should begin with a**

first-line indent and no extra space between paragraphs. Extra white space often signals a self-published look and disrupts the natural flow of reading. Exceptions are seen in self-help books.

Think of it this way: a book that's over-spaced feels more like a typed-up Word document than a professionally printed book. If you want your work to sit comfortably next to traditionally published books, this small detail matters.

INDENTATION

This topic is sometimes controversial, so I'll share my research and let you decide what works best for your book.

Indentation is the small space at the beginning of a paragraph that separates it visually from the previous one. It's a small detail, but it significantly impacts how professional and easy-to-read your book feels. While traditional print books almost always use indentation, modern nonfiction sometimes skips indenting the first paragraph after a chapter title or subheading for a cleaner, contemporary look.

While we don't have time to get into all the rules that apply to indentation standards, below are a few best practices that can be useful.

Best Practices:

- **Traditional Rule:** Indent every paragraph (standard 0.25–0.5 inches, with 0.3 being common).
- **Nonfiction Style:** Skip the indent for the first paragraph after titles or headings, but keep this choice consistent throughout the book.
- **eBooks:** Indentation is often applied automatically, but always check the preview file to avoid awkward spacing.

Consistency is what matters most. Whether you indent every paragraph or follow the modern nonfiction style, choose one approach and stick with it, random formatting screams "self-published."

PAGE NUMBERS AND HEADERS

Page numbers and headers are small details, but they speak volumes about professionalism. Always include **page numbers**, since readers rely on them for navigation. However, skip numbering on the title page and on chapter-opening pages. This keeps the layout clean and consistent with industry standards.

For an added professional touch, include **headers or footers** with either your book title or your author name. This is what you'll see in traditionally published books, and it instantly elevates the look of your work.

As a resource, view the "Formatting Standards Guide" I created for you in the Resources section. It outlines the dos and don'ts of formatting in one place, so you can double-check your work before publishing.

CHAPTER TITLES

Chapter titles set the tone for what's to come, so they need to be clean, professional, and consistently formatted. They also help create a smooth reading experience and give your book a polished, bookstore-ready feel.

Best Practices:

- Placement: Always start each chapter on a right-hand (recto) page, this is the publishing standard and immediately makes your book look professional.

- **Formatting:** Center the chapter title, using **bold** or **all caps** for clarity and emphasis.
- Numbering: Keep chapter numbers consistent (either spelled out, CHAPTER THREE, or numeric, CHAPTER 3).
- **Spacing:** Leave enough white space before and after the title to give it room to breathe (usually ⅓ of the page before the title).

Below is an example of how you can format the chapter number and title to support your publishing needs.

Example:

CHAPTER THREE

Defining Your Purpose & Reader

MARGINS & GUTTERS

Margins and gutters are the invisible framework that keeps your book readable and professional. They determine how close your text is to the edges of the page and how much space is left in the spine (gutter). Getting this wrong can ruin your reader's experience.

Below, I also want to share a couple of best practices that have saved me more than a few headaches.

First, always use your publishing platform's templates, whether that's Amazon KDP, IngramSpark, or D2D. These templates are designed to account for trim size, page count, and binding type. In other words, all the technical details you don't want to leave to guesswork.

Second, pay close attention to your margins. I can't count how many self-published books I've seen where the text disappears into the spine or runs so close to the page edge that it's hard to read. Nothing screams "self-published" louder than a book that makes readers struggle with the layout.

For thicker books, gutter space increases automatically in professional templates to allow for the curve of the spine, another reason to trust the provided specs.

PUBLISHING TIP

Before you hit publish, protect your reputation by doing two simple but critical things:

1. **Download the official templates from the distributor before designing:** Templates calculate spine width, trim size, and margins automatically, which helps prevent costly formatting mistakes.
2. **Order a printed proof copy:** Take the time to check for ink smears, paper quality, and spacing issues page by page. Readers notice these details, and one overlooked mistake can lead to bad reviews you can't erase. Your book deserves better, and so do your readers.

When I tried to format my first cover on Amazon KDP, it felt like a nightmare. No matter what I did, the system kept rejecting it. After several frustrating attempts, I finally realized the issue was with my trim size. Because the page count had changed, the spine measurement had changed, too. Fortunately, Amazon KDP has a tool that flags these mismatches so you can correct them right away. IngramSpark, however, works differently. If the same type of error happens there, you may not know the cause for several days, which can delay your ability to publish. Experiences like these are why formatting and covers go hand in hand, getting one right ensures the other fits.

And the next chapter will give you greater insight into the impact of book covers and why they matter so much in self-publishing. Let us explore what I call the Wonderful World of Book Covers.

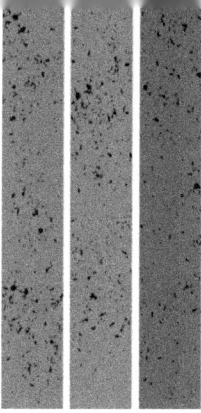

CHAPTER 9
THE WONDERFUL WORLD OF BOOK COVERS

THERE ARE SO MANY THINGS I wish I had known early on about book covers. It would have saved me so much time and energy. From understanding how covers need to align with your genre, to proper title placement, to choosing the right front and back cover design options, there's far more to a book cover than most first-time authors realize.

Over my publishing career, I've designed or consulted on multiple book covers. Now, with every single one, I ask a magical question:

"If I saw this on a bookshelf, would it make me want to pick it up?"

If the answer is "no," we're not there yet, and more work needs to be done. And trust me, you shouldn't settle for "good enough" either. It has the potential to haunt you if you don't push for something great. Your book cover is the first impression readers have of your work, and in many cases, it determines whether they ever read a single word you've written.

THE AIRPORT SHELF TEST

When publishing *Oakland Hills, Milwaukee Rivers* (First Edition), I wanted a vibrant book cover that reflected the symbolism woven throughout the book and the story itself. I contracted a cover designer on Fiverr and shared my ideas, and he began to provide mock-ups. My thoughts and ideas came to life.

But one day, while traveling back from San Diego with a layover in Nashville, I wandered into one of those airport bookstands. I always stop at airport bookstands for two reasons: (1) to see what's on the bestseller list, and (2) to study what the book covers look like, because as a self-published author, you must fit in with the books that are already selling visually.

Our dream as self-publishing authors is to see our books in stores, on airport shelves, or even floating across a commercial. This day, I wanted to see if my book *looked* like it belonged on a bestseller's shelf.

I remember standing there, scanning the books: Melania's book was on display, Tina Knowles's *Matriarch* was right next to it, and Mel Robbins's *The Let Them Theory* stood out with its bold, professional design. I slowly pulled my book from my bag, placed it on the shelf, stepped back, and for a moment, I simply stared. Then, I snapped a photo, smiling like a kid on Christmas morning.

Even though I didn't have a fancy distribution company to place it there, for that moment, it *felt* like it belonged. But here's the truth: **it didn't**. My book, as beautiful as it looked, stood out but not in the same way as the bestsellers on that shelf. While it was my vision, I accepted the truth and moved forward. It was, and still is, different from the books around it, but I chose to own my decision to be symbolic instead of fitting the memoir aesthetic.

When it comes to your book cover, **you must ask yourself the same question and be okay with the answer**:

"If my book were sitting next to the bestsellers in my genre, would it look like it belonged, or would it stand out for the wrong reasons?"

Your cover isn't a creative choice, it's a business decision. It's the single most powerful marketing tool you have, and readers will judge it in less than three seconds. Those are publishing facts. If it looks amateurish, many will assume the writing is too. But if it looks professional, genre-appropriate, and eye-catching, you've already won half the battle.

GENRE ALIGNMENT: DOES YOUR COVER FIT IN?

Here's a simple rule: **Your cover should fit in while standing out.** It should look like it belongs in your genre, but it should also have a unique element that catches the eye. Consider this if you're writing this book type:

- **Memoir:** Readers expect emotional tones, clean typography, and often an image that reflects the story's theme (not a random smiling headshot).
- **Self-Help/Leadership:** Bold titles, clear fonts, and a color palette that conveys authority and trust.
- **Inspirational/Religious:** Warm, inviting tones that suggest hope and transformation.

A big mistake I see in self-publishing is authors trying to be too different, picking fonts, colors, or layouts that don't match their genre. As a result, readers get confused about the book's genre and skip right past it.

I encourage you to go look at 10–15 bestsellers in your genre. What colors do they use? What's the font style? Where is the title placed? Use those as *guidelines,* not to copy, but to understand what readers subconsciously expect. I go to Barnes & Noble frequently for this reason.

THE ANATOMY OF A BOOK COVER

A professional cover is more than looking good; it's about ensuring every detail works together to draw readers in.

Here's what you need to know:

- **Front Cover:** Your first impression. It should have a clear title, an easy-to-read subtitle (if applicable), your name, and visuals that fit your genre. If someone wouldn't pick it up at first glance, it likely needs more work.
- **Spine**: What people see first on a shelf. Make sure your title and name are centered, easy to read, and not cramped.
- **Back Cover:** Where the sale happens. A short, compelling book blurb, your author bio or photo, and your ISBN/barcode go here. If you have endorsements, this is where they shine.
- **Inner Flaps (for jacketed hardcovers):** Bonus space for reviews, extended bio, or a call-to-action, but not required for paperbacks or eBooks.

Remember, a sloppy cover screams amateur, but a clean, professional one signals to readers that what's inside is worth their time.

TYPES OF BOOK COVERS YOU NEED TO KNOW

Before we get too deep into design tips, let's talk about the types of covers you might need. Each format has its requirements, and understanding them early can save you a lot of headaches later.

1. **eBook Cover:** This is the simplest format because it's digital-only. You're designing the front cover, no spine, no back. The key here is clarity. Your cover needs to stand out as a thumbnail because most people will see it first on Amazon or another

digital platform. Clean fonts, high contrast, and bold images are essential.

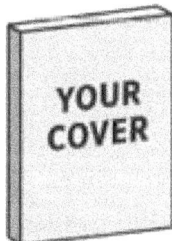

2. **Paperback Cover:** A paperback cover includes the front, spine, and back. This means you need to account for more than making it look good, your spine width changes depending on how many pages your book has, and your back cover needs space for a blurb, author bio, and ISBN barcode. Paperbacks are the most common format for self-publishing because they're affordable to print and easy to distribute.

3. **Hardcover Cover:** A hardcover cover is more expensive to produce than a paperback but feels premium in readers' hands. It can either be a "case laminate" (printed directly onto the hardboard cover) or come with a separate jacket. Hardcovers are often used for books you want to position as collectible, premium, or gift-worthy, think leadership, business, or coffee table books.

4. **Jacketed (Dust Jacket) Hardcover:** This is the most traditional format you'll see in bookstores. The hardcover itself is plain or has a minimal printed design, and a removable paper jacket wraps around it. The jacket includes flaps where you can add additional text, author photos, or marketing blurbs. This option is more expensive and is best if you're positioning your book for bookstores or want that classic, professional feel. However, this option is considered integral to the book as an art object.

YOUR COVER — EBOOK COVER

YOUR COVER — PAPERBACK COVER

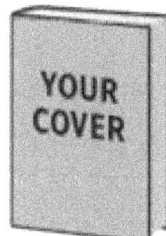

YOUR COVER — HARDCOVER COVER

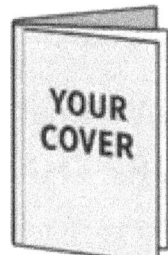

YOUR COVER — JACKETED (DUST JACKET) HARDCOVER

BOOK SIZES AND TEMPLATES: WHY THEY MATTER

Before starting the cover design, it's important to decide on the book size (also called the 'trim size'). The most common sizes for nonfiction and memoirs are:

- **5 x 8 inches**: Great for portability, often used for memoirs.
- **5.5 x 8.5 inches:** A popular choice for self-help and nonfiction.
- **6 x 9 inches:** The standard trade paperback size, ideal for most nonfiction books.

Each platform, Amazon KDP, D2D, and IngramSpark, has specific templates you must use to ensure your cover fits perfectly. These templates take into account your trim size, spine width (based on page count), and barcode placement.

If you don't follow the exact template, your book can be rejected during upload, or worse, your cover might print misaligned.

The good news is that the templates are free. You can download them directly from the platform you plan to publish on. And yes, YouTube has endless step-by-step videos showing you how to use them.

For a more detailed, step-by-step publishing guide, I'll have a downloadable resource available on my website to walk you through this process.

WHY YOUR COVER MATTERS MORE THAN YOU THINK

Until I got into self-publishing, I didn't realize a hard truth. People *do* judge books by their covers. Literally, from the color, who is on the cover, to the title, and to what you say, or don't say, on the back of your book cover. It all matters.

Recently, I was online and came across a book by a young woman on the East Coast who had become a new author. Her cover was vibrant and full of color, with a perfectly aligned title and a professional-looking photo of her. I was intrigued and wanted to know more about her book, so I zoomed in on the image, flipped to the back cover, and started reading the description.

That was when I noticed it, an incomplete sentence. It stopped me mid-read, leaving me unable to grasp what the story was about fully. In that moment, the book felt unfinished, and her credibility, at least to me as a reader, was diminished.

I reached out to let her know because I believe we have a responsibility as fellow authors to help each other. That's also why this book was written, to help you, to help us, and to empower others.

Why does this matter? Because what we share with the world is an extension of ourselves. When we design book covers, front or back, we must ensure they meet professional standards. Every detail counts, and readers notice more than we think.

A professional-looking cover says three things:

1. **This book is worth my money.**
2. **This author is serious and credible.**
3. **This is the kind of book I love to read.**

A poorly designed cover says the opposite, before anyone reads a single word. Especially as self-published authors, and like it or not, your book cover sets that expectation before anyone even flips to the first page.

WRITING A BACK COVER BLURB THAT SELLS

You've formatted your manuscript, identified your cover design process, and solidified what the front cover will look like. But now, let's talk about the back cover blurb, the part of your book that will convince readers to buy it.

Think of your back cover blurb as your **book's elevator pitch**. It's not a complete summary of your book, and it's not where you explain every detail. It's a carefully crafted teaser designed to spark curiosity and make the reader say, *I need this book.*

During my first publishing attempt, I made the mistake of writing my back cover blurb like a journal entry. It felt personal, but it didn't tell potential readers why they should care. By the second edition, I understood something important: your back cover isn't for you, it's for them.

Based on my mistakes, observations, and research from over the years, here are some best practices to follow:

- **Lead with a Hook:** Start with one or two sentences that grab attention. Ask a thought-provoking question or make a bold statement that speaks to your reader's pain point or desire. (Example: "Have you ever felt trapped between who you are and who the world expects you to be?").
- **Focus on the Reader's Transformation**: Don't **just** tell them what's in the book; tell them what it will do for them. Use this simple formula: "This book will help you [solve a problem or achieve a goal] by [key benefit]."
- **Keep It Tight:** 150 words or less. Readers scanning your book in a store don't want to read a long essay.
- **Write Like a Marketer, Not Like an Author:** Remember, this isn't where you tell your life story. It's a sales tool. Speak directly to your target audience. Include Social Proof or a

- **Credibility Line (if possible):** If you have a notable achievement, quote, or endorsement, add a one-line credibility statement. *(Example: "Dr. Keyimani Alford, leadership expert and bestselling author of Unshaken Leadership...").*
- **End with a Call to Action:** Encourage them to take the next step. *(Example: "Your story matters. Start reclaiming it today.")*

DIY VS. HIRING A PROFESSIONAL

Can you design your own cover? Technically, yes. Should you? Probably not, unless you have professional design experience. As a self-publishing author, this is not the time to practice your graphic design skills, especially if you want to sell books.

Pay a professional to design your cover, and pay them what they're worth. A skilled designer understands spacing, font hierarchy, color theory, and genre expectations. Your cousin, who is "good at Canva," doesn't.

Now, don't get me wrong, some amazing things can be done with Canva. In fact, I originally designed this book cover in Canva. The difference? I have years of graphic design experience and have spent hours studying what makes a strong book cover.

There are rules to cover design, and breaking them without understanding them can cost you credibility and sales. For example, if your cover isn't legible at thumbnail size, readers may never click. Or if your imagery and typography don't match your genre, you risk losing the audience before they even read your description. But hiring a pro doesn't mean throwing money at the first person you find. Here are some tips on making informed choices.

HOW TO HIRE A DESIGNER

To increase your chances of hiring the right designer, these tips will guide you before, during, and after the process.

- **Request samples:** Make sure the designer has experience in your genre. For my first book, I put out a call on Facebook for a cover designer, and many people responded. But here's the thing, not all of them designed book covers. Some were simply reusing other people's designs and passing them off as their own.

- **Validate work before hiring:** Look up the books they claim to have designed, check Amazon, Barnes & Noble, or other credible websites to confirm the cover is published and associated with that author. If they can't show you real, verifiable examples of their work, that's a red flag.

- **Check reviews**: Fiverr, Reedsy, and 99designs have credible designers, but always verify their portfolios and the comments of others who have used their services. Doing this often can save you time and money.

- **Request a mock-up**: Many designers will do a sample concept for a small fee. This is your project, and if they want your business, they will do what is necessary to make you a customer.

- **Get a contract**: Never pay 100% upfront. Whenever possible, pay in installments as milestones are completed. Services like Fiverr require full payment upfront, but it's typically processed through PayPal, which adds another layer of protection if something goes wrong.

- **Treat people right:** I've worked with enough professional designers to know that many reputable ones will begin work before payment is received, especially once they've established a credible working relationship with you. If a designer insists on full payment before even starting, and you can't verify their track record, proceed with caution.

COST EXPECTATION

Prices will always vary depending on the designer and their demand. However, there are some average costs associated with book covers. It is recommended that you budget:

- **$100–$300** for eBook-only covers.
- **$250–$600** for full paperback wrap-around covers (front, spine, and back).

Yes, that might feel expensive, but remember: Your cover is your most important marketing tool. A quality book cover will be the best investment you'll make to get the attention of the reader.

MISTAKES TO AVOID

Several factors should be considered when designing or outsourcing your book cover. Utilize these tips as you consider what is best to promote your book visually.

- **Too much text:** Your primary title should be 3–6 words in length, maximum. Too much text on your front cover makes it look busy and unprofessional
- **Your title doesn't match what your book is about**: People ignore your book and fail to purchase it.
- **Not considering Search Engine Optimization (SEO):** Readers need to find your book when searching for specific keywords. This does not mean stuffing the cover with text, but it does mean using clear, concise titles and subtitles that reflect the language readers are likely to type into a search bar.

- **Avoid clutter in your cover design:** A crowded layout distracts from the title, makes the book look unprofessional, and reduces its impact both online and in print.
- **Prevent overcomplicated graphics:** Simple sells.
- **Tiny fonts:** If you can't read it in a thumbnail, neither can readers shopping on Amazon.
- **Not checking print bleed and trim size:** This is a common pitfall. Always follow Amazon KDP or IngramSpark guidelines for proper dimensions. A lack of understanding here can become a significant barrier to launching your book. Amazon KDP is generally easier to work with, but IngramSpark can be painful at times.

Understanding these mistakes will help you be better prepared when designing your own cover or when outsourcing this. The more you know, the better your design will be.

YOUR TURN: COVER AUDIT EXERCISE

Take a moment to do this:

1. Pull up 10 bestselling books in your genre on Amazon.
2. Write down three things they all have in common (fonts, colors, title size, etc.).
3. Write down one unique element you want your cover to have.
4. Ask yourself: **If my book were sitting next to these, would it fit in?**

Keep this list handy when you start working with your designer or creating your own mock-ups.

LESSON LEARNED: YOUR COVER IS YOUR SILENT SALESPERSON

Your cover works for you when you're not in the room. It's the first thing people see, and it will either invite them in or push them away.

Don't rush this step.

When I held my polished copy of my book for the first time, it wasn't just the story inside that made me proud, it was knowing the book looked professional enough to stand alongside the best. This is what I want for you, too.

CHAPTER 10
THE FINAL
PREPARATION CHECKLIST

YOU HAVE WRITTEN YOUR BOOK, polished your manuscript, and designed a cover that looks professional. Now it's time for the final step that takes your book from your desk to the hands of readers: distribution. But before you can make it available to the world, you need to handle a few professional essentials, things that determine how legitimate your book looks, how easily people can find it, and how well it's protected.

Initially, I had no idea this part existed. For years, I read books without ever paying attention to the details behind them. For me, it was always the title and the author's name, I never once considered the ISBN, the copyright page, or the Library of Congress Control Number.

It wasn't until I was ready to publish my own book that I realized how much I didn't know. I had to research every step, figure out how to navigate multiple systems, and make numerous mistakes along the way. And let me tell you, it wasn't easy. There was a lot to learn, and simply understanding how all the pieces worked together took time and patience.

The good news for you is that I've already done the trial and error, so you don't have to. All the essential information is right here in one place. When I started, the information was scattered throughout, and I wasted hours redoing things because I had uploaded something incorrectly or formatted a section incorrectly.

This is where attention to detail matters, a lot. If you get this part wrong, it can delay your book's release or even stop it from being published altogether. Think of this step as the domino that sets everything else in motion. Get it right, and you'll set yourself, and your book, up for success.

I know this all too well. When I was publishing one of my books and going through the copyright phase, I thought I could submit two publications simultaneously—only to later find out I couldn't. The copyright system allows just one transmission at a time, even though it appears to let you submit multiple. This mistake caused a three-week delay and required multiple emails and several hours of research to resolve.

WHAT WE'LL COVER IN THIS CHAPTER

By the end of this chapter, you'll understand the critical elements and processes that pertain to the following publishing elements:

- **ISBNs (International Standard Book Numbers):** What they are, why you need them, how much they cost, and how to purchase them in the United States of America (US).
- **Copyrights:** What copyright protection does (and doesn't) do, how to register your book, and what to include in a professional copyright page.
- **Library of Congress Control Numbers (LCCN):** What they are, whether you need one, and how to apply.
- **Metadata:** What it means, why it's critical for your book's discoverability, and how to set it up correctly.
- **Best Practices:** Tips to avoid costly mistakes (like the one I made) and make this process smoother.

My advice to you? Take your time with these processes. Each step is crucial to your book's success, and rushing through them can cost you valuable time, and potentially money.

ISBNS: YOUR BOOK'S UNIQUE IDENTIFIER

What is an ISBN?

An ISBN (International Standard Book Number) is your book's fingerprint, a 13-digit code used by booksellers, libraries, and distributors to track and sell your book. If you want your book to look professional and be searchable in databases, you need one.

Here are reasons why you might need one:

- **eBooks on Amazon:** Amazon gives you an **ASIN** (Amazon Standard Identification Number). You don't need to purchase an ISBN unless you plan to distribute your book outside of Amazon.
- **Print Books (Paperback & Hardcover):** Yes. Each version, paperback, hardcover, and eBook, needs its own ISBN.

Where to Get One in the United States:

- **Bowker (Official U.S. ISBN Agency):** www.myidentifiers.com
  - **Cost:** $125 for one ISBN or $295 for a pack of 10 (recommended if you plan multiple books or formats).
- **Free ISBNs (Amazon KDP & D2D):** Convenient, but they list **Amazon or the distributor as the publisher**, not you.

Once you apply and pay for your ISBN, it will be assigned to you and added to your profile. Within your profile, you'll see the 13-digit number that you'll assign to the specific book format (eBook, paperback, or hardcover). It's recommended to allow at least 24–48 hours for the ISBN to be registered and fully recognized in industry databases. You can still add the ISBN to your copyright page and publishing system during this time, but please note that the metadata may not update immediately.

Self-Publishing Advice: If you're serious about building a publishing brand, like I did with Keywords Unlocked Publishers, buy your own ISBNs. This not only looks more professional but also gives you complete control and reinforces your credibility as a self-publishing author.

Owning your ISBNs allows you to sell your book on multiple platforms without being tied to a single distributor's system.

COPYRIGHT: PROTECTING YOUR WORK

Protecting your work is a crucial step you should take. It secures your right to defend the intellectual property you've spent many hours creating. If you skip this step, or do it wrong, you risk losing proof that your content is legally yours.

UNDERSTANDING WHAT YOU ALREADY OWN

Technically, the moment you write your manuscript, it's automatically copyrighted. However, if someone plagiarizes your work, you need official registration to have legal protection to enforce your rights in court.

When copyrighting your work, the cost varies. As a self-publishing author with one work, you'll pay $45.00. If others contribute, like a publisher, co-author, or editor, the price increases.

Copyrighting in general matters, because without registration, you can't pursue statutory damages or attorney's fees if someone infringes on your work. Think of this as **insurance for your intellectual property**.

As you prepared your manuscript, you had to create the "front matter." This includes items such as the copyright page, dedication, quotes, table of contents, and publications. One crucial element is the copyright page. It traditionally appears on the left-hand page, directly after the full title page. In publishing, this is called the verso page, but all you need to remember is that the copyright page always follows the title page.

Because this page is so critical, I wanted to include a copy of a simple standard format of what this looks like again. Use this as your template.

A SAMPLE PROFESSIONAL COPYRIGHT PAGE

I mentioned this earlier, but it deserves repeating because of how critical it is to get right. An example is included here and again in the Resources section. For ISBNs and LCCNs, you will receive a unique identifier when you apply.

Copyright © 2025 by Bestselling Author

The Self-Publishing from Scratch Book
All rights reserved. No part of this book may be reproduced, stored in a retrieval system, or transmitted in any form or by any means, electronic, mechanical, photocopying, recording, or otherwise, without the prior written permission of the publisher, except for brief quotations in reviews or articles.

Printed in the United States of America by Bestseller Publishing

ISBN (Paperback): 978-1-234567-89-0
ISBN (eBook): 978-1-234567-89-0

LCCN: 9876543210

For information, visit: www.bestseller.com

Self-Publishing Advice: The easiest way to copyright your book (in the U.S.) is through the official website at **www.copyright.gov**. The filing fee is $45–$65. You'll complete the online registration form, upload a PDF copy of your book, and then wait for processing. Most authors receive their certificate within three to eight months.

METADATA: HELPING READERS FIND YOU

WHAT IS METADATA?

Metadata is the **behind-the-scenes data** about your book that makes it searchable online. It includes:

- Title & Subtitle
- Author Name (exactly as it appears on your cover)
- ISBN
- Keywords & Categories
- Book Description / Blurb

WHAT DOES METADATA DO?

When someone searches for "self-publishing for beginners" or "healing from childhood trauma," your metadata determines whether your book appears.

Because metadata relies on keywords for your book to be found, you need to be strategic in this process. Here's some preliminary advice to support your success, with detailed insight provided in Chapter 15.

- Use all **seven keyword slots** the distributor allows.
- Be accurate with your categories, don't mislead readers to hit a bestseller list.
- Think like your reader: "What would they type to find a book like mine?"

LESSON LEARNED: DON'T SKIP THIS STEP

When releasing a book, you may consider a free ISBN to save costs, but realize it will limit distribution on other platforms. I was lucky and avoided that problem early, but unlike many authors, some don't, and lose full control of their work.

Learn from me: Invest in your own ISBNs. Register your copyright upfront. This is more than looking professional; it's about maintaining control, building credibility, and safeguarding your legacy. These decisions may seem small now, but they have long-term consequences for how your book is perceived in the world.

Now that you've taken ownership of your book's identity, its ISBN, its metadata, and its legal protection, it's time to make the next big decision: Where will you publish it?

This next phase is all about access and alignment. Your publishing path determines how your book reaches readers, how much you'll earn, and how much freedom you'll have. Whether you choose Amazon KDP, IngramSpark, a hybrid service, or multiple channels, each option comes with its own trade-offs.

In the next chapter, I'll help you evaluate your goals, understand your options, and choose the publishing route that best suits *your* needs.

Let's move from protection to positioning to get your book into the world, the right way, and the next chapter will help us do that.

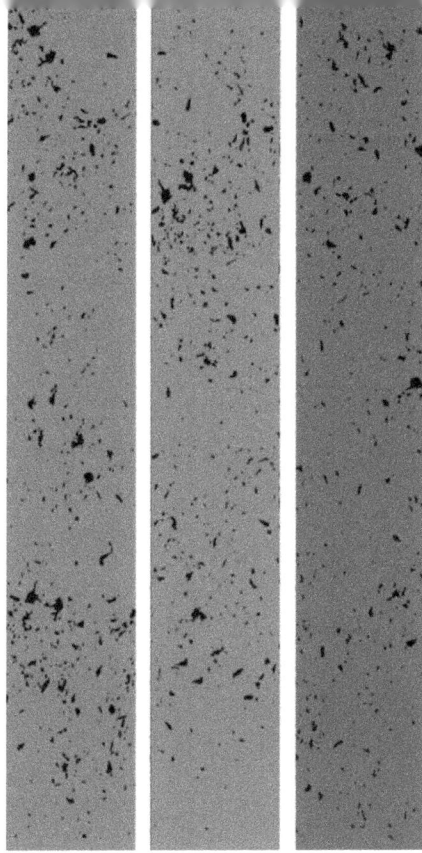

PART THREE: PRESENTATION
PRODUCTION & PUBLISHING

CHAPTER 11
DETERMINING WHERE TO PUBLISH

THIS IS IT, the moment where everything you've worked on finally meets the world. Your ideas, your story, your lessons... all packaged into a book that will represent you. But here's the hard truth: What you publish is your brand, credibility, and the legacy you'll leave behind.

And legacies aren't built on "good enough."

Industry reports show that 81% of published authors in the U.S. are White, while the percentage of Black authors ranges from 5% to 7%. This disparity isn't just a statistic; it's a reminder that for those of us who are minorities in this industry, our work will be scrutinized even more. People will judge the quality of your book before they ever open it.

Honestly, ask yourself: "Is what I created good enough to proudly sit on the shelf next to anyone else's work?" Because it must be, your name is on it. Your future opportunities might depend on it. And long after you're gone, this book will represent you. Make sure it represents you well.

Distribution is where all your hard work finally comes to life. But I've learned that not all distribution platforms are created equal. The platform you choose to publish on can affect how much control you keep, how much money you make, and how widely your book is available.

In this chapter, I'll share insights into this process. While many platforms are available, I'll focus on three major ones, those you often hear about in YouTube videos: Amazon KDP, IngramSpark, and D2D. These are popular, but if you want to learn more about other platforms like Lulu and Barnes & Noble Press, you can find additional information online.

When determining whether to publish, it depends on what book you're going to publish and if you want a global or U.S.-based distribution. I have learned through my publishing journey that some platforms offer you a greater benefit than others, so take your time to review this content to make the decision on what is best for you.

AMAZON KDP

Amazon KDP is a self-publishing platform for eBooks, paperbacks, and hardcover books. With Amazon controlling over 70% of the U.S. eBook market, it's a must-have platform for most self-publishing authors. But here's what many people don't realize: there's a process happening behind the scenes that you must complete before your book can go public.

The first thing to understand is that you're not publishing through "Amazon," you're publishing through Amazon KDP. You need to create a separate account, different from your regular Amazon shopping account, specifically for publishing. I didn't know this when I first started, and it led to unnecessary delays.

To save you time, I've outlined the primary steps you need to take below. This isn't a full tutorial, but it will give you the foundational knowledge to answer two of the most important questions: **Where do I go?** and **What do I need to get started?**

Before You Upload:

- Proofread and format your manuscript (PDF for print, DOCX or EPUB for eBook).
- Have a high-resolution cover (Amazon KDP template recommended).
- Use the free Amazon KDP ISBN, but note it lists Amazon as the publisher, which might limit control and credibility. For full ownership and flexibility, purchase your own as mentioned earlier from Bowker.
- Have your details ready, like your book title (including subtitle), description, author bio, total pages, imprint name, categories (e.g., biography, memoir, self-help), and SEO keywords.
- Set up your business info and create your profile in the system for payment and distribution. Have your business details (name, EIN or SSN, address) and financial info ready for direct deposits.

Uploading Steps:

1. Go to **https://kdp.amazon.com/**
2. Create or log into your Amazon KDP account.
3. Choose "Paperback," "Hardcover," or "Kindle eBook."
4. Enter book details (title, subtitle, author, keywords, categories).
5. Upload interior file & cover (follow Amazon KDP's trim size template).
6. Set pricing & royalties (Amazon KDP provides a calculator).
7. Order a proof copy before approving for publication.

To be fully transparent with you, there are some advantages and disadvantages of using Amazon KDP, and I've outlined some of them in the chart within the Resources section of the book.

Self-Publishing Advice: Use Amazon KDP, but if you're building your own author or publishing brand, you might find it more beneficial to buy your own ISBNs for professionalism and flexibility.

Why does this matter? Because if you use Amazon's free ISBN, you can only publish your book on Amazon's platform. If you want to distribute your book elsewhere, such as IngramSpark, D2D, or bookstores, you need to own yours.

Bottom Line: If you want control of your publishing rights and the ability to expand your reach, invest in your own ISBN. If you're only publishing on Amazon and don't mind their name being listed as the publisher, the free option may work. But remember, this is your legacy, and every choice you make reflects your brand.

INGRAMSPARK

IngramSpark is a global distribution platform for print books and is trusted by bookstores and libraries worldwide. If you want your book on the shelves of Barnes & Noble, Books-A-Million, or in libraries, IngramSpark is the way to go. It gives self-publishing authors a wide distribution opportunity that other platforms don't. However, like every service, there are some disadvantages to using it. Don't worry if this feels like a lot of information, I break it down visually in the Resources section so you can clearly see the pros and cons side by side.

One of the biggest lessons I learned with IngramSpark is that it automatically feeds into Amazon for print books. This is great news if you want your hardcover jacketed book (dust jacket) available on Amazon, because once it's live on IngramSpark, it will appear there too.

I learned this the hard way. One year, I created a hardcover version on Amazon and a jacketed hardcover version on

IngramSpark. This caused significant confusion because I didn't understand the integration process. I wanted readers to buy the jacketed version, but it required too many clicks and forced me to send people to multiple websites. Later, I found out IngramSpark integrates with Amazon, so readers can buy your hardcover directly there. I had wasted time setting up the Amazon hardcover and eventually deleted it so IngramSpark could push my jacketed version through.

This small insight changed my entire approach. Now, I know how to maximize both platforms, especially since Amazon remains the largest book retailer in the United States.

Here's my personal or professional opinion: if you're going to publish a hardcover, choose the jacketed version, as it adds a premium feel and traditional appeal. However, this is ultimately your decision. Amazon's hardcover option is cheaper to produce, but you sacrifice quality for cost.

Just like with Amazon KDP, you'll need to **create an account** and learn IngramSpark's system. Each platform has its own quirks and requirements, and you'll need to familiarize yourself with its process before publishing.

As you prepare to use this platform, here is where you go and what you need to get started with IngramSpark:

Before You Upload:
- You *should* have your own ISBN purchased from Bowker.
- You must have your final formatted PDF for print.
- Cover with IngramSpark's spine width & bleed specifications.
- If you're doing the jacketed cover, you will need the manuscript, your regular cover (front, back, spine), and your jacketed cover design (front, back, spine, right flap, left flap).

- Have your details ready: This includes your book title (both primary and subtitle), book description, author bio, total page count, publishing imprint name, book categories (e.g., biography, self-help, memoir, nonfiction), and SEO-friendly keywords.
- Set up your business information: If you're uploading for the first time, you'll need to establish your business profile in the system for payment and distribution. Be prepared with your business information (name, EIN or SSN, and address) as well as your financial details for direct deposits.

Uploading Steps:

1. Go to **https://www.ingramspark.com/**
2. Create an IngramSpark account.
3. Enter metadata (ensure it matches Amazon KDP for consistency).
4. Upload print-ready files.
5. Set wholesale discount (45–55%) & returnability (many bookstores prefer returnable books).

Self-Publishing Advice: Use IngramSpark + Amazon KDP together for maximum reach. While I might mention this later in this chapter, it's important to mention it here. While there is no initial setup fee, after 60 days, any changes to your manuscript or cover come with a cost.

While IngramSpark is often the go-to for print distribution, D2D shines when it comes to eBooks.

DRAFT2DIGITAL (D2D)

Draft2Digital is also a popular book distributor, but its strength primarily lies in the eBook market. While it now offers print-on-demand options, that feature is still relatively new to the platform.

When I first published, I used D2D for both eBook and print. However, I quickly learned that I was **duplicating services** by using multiple distributors for the same formats. This is an important lesson for you as a self-publishing author: pay close attention to which platform does what best, and **intertwine them strategically** to create the best publishing experience.

For eBooks, D2D has been my go-to. Its global reach extends beyond Amazon, distributing to platforms such as Apple Books, Kobo, Barnes & Noble Nook, and Scribd, a huge advantage if you want to reach readers Amazon doesn't always reach. Over time, I found this particularly valuable for my subsequent eBook publications.

Additionally, if you take the time to learn the system, D2D offers tools that make the process easier. Here are some of those tools:

- **ePub Conversion Tool**: D2D converts your manuscript into a proper ePub file, which is the format required to sell your eBook on most platforms.
- **Universal Book Link (UBL)**: UBL lets you create a single link where all your books across platforms are listed in one central location. Trust me, this is a game-changer when managing multiple distributors.

We are friends here, right? No gatekeeping, remember. The platform may not be the most visually appealing, but it gets the job done. More importantly, it's one of the best options for eBook distribution, which makes it worth using.

If you're considering print, you can order author copies without that glaring Amazon "not for resale" stripe across them. However, be prepared for delays, it can take several weeks to receive them.

Like the other platforms, you'll need to create a free account, but be mindful of post-publication changes. D2D charges a $25 fee per change after 90 days of publishing in "change tokens" so finalize as much as you can before hitting that publish button.

Before You Upload:

- Upload a clean EPUB or DOCX file (you can use D2D's basic formatting tool).
- Upload a professional eBook cover (JPG, 1600x2560 px or larger).
- Prepare your details: This includes your book title (both primary and subtitle), book description, author bio, total page count, publishing imprint name, book categories (e.g., biography, self-help, memoir, nonfiction), and SEO-friendly keywords.
- Set up your business information: If uploading for the first time to establish your profile for payment and distribution. Have your business name, EIN or SSN, address, and financial details ready.

Uploading Steps:

1. Go to **https://draft2digital.com/**
2. Create a D2D account.
3. Enter book details & upload manuscript.
4. Use D2D's template or upload your own formatted file.
5. Select platforms to distribute to (Apple Books, Kobo, Nook, Scribd).
6. Approve the preview & set pricing.

Self-Publishing Advice: Use D2D for eBooks if you want to expand outside Amazon but don't want the complexity of managing multiple platforms individually.

This section was designed to give you a clear, practical overview of what you need to successfully upload your files, create your accounts, and navigate the major publishing platforms with confidence. It's not meant to be an exhaustive, step-by-step tutorial, those guides are coming soon, where I'll walk you through every click of the process. But what you have here is enough to move forward without feeling completely lost or overwhelmed.

My goal is to help you avoid the same trial-and-error frustrations I went through, so you can focus on getting your book into readers' hands quickly.

As you decide which platform to use, consider what each one does best strategically. Not all distributors are equal, some excel in eBook distribution, while others dominate in print or offer wider bookstore and library access. Choosing the right combination can maximize your reach and keep your publishing process efficient.

To help you make that decision, there is a "Book Publishing Pros and Cons Checklist" to assist you in the Resources section. Use it as a guide to compare platforms briefly so you can make the best decision for your book and your long-term goals as a self-publishing author.

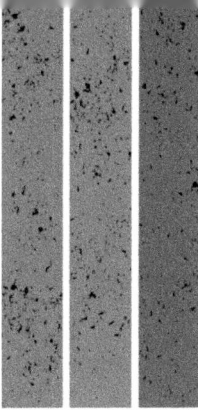

CHAPTER 12
THE SERVICE EXPERIENCE

ONE THING I FELT WAS IMPORTANT to share in this book is the actual experience of using these platforms. Yes, you're a self-publishing author, navigating most of this on your own, besides having this guide to help you (good job, by the way!). But you're not only an author; you're also a customer of the platform you choose. And with that role come real experiences—both good and bad—you need to be prepared for.

I've watched countless YouTubers who rant about how terrible some platforms are, and others who swear by them. I've even seen videos titled, *"Stop Selling Your Books on Amazon!"* trying to convince authors to jump to another distributor in the name of "global reach."

Ignore the hype. If you decide to handle this entire process yourself, you need to understand exactly what you're getting into, not what someone online is yelling about. My goal isn't to steer you away from any platform due to a bad personal experience, but to help you make informed decisions.

In this section, I focus on five key areas you need to know before jumping full force into using the distributor platforms:

- Uploading your book
- Getting author copies
- Customer service

- Audience reach
- Book templates

These may sound simple, but trust me, they can give you a migraine if you don't know what to expect.

For clarity, this chapter is based on my experiences with **Amazon KDP, IngramSpark**, and **D2D**, three major players in self-publishing.

Choosing where to distribute your book is important. Each platform comes with unique strengths, limitations, and quirks that can directly impact your experience as a self-publishing author. Below is a comparison of three major players, Amazon KDP, IngramSpark, and D2D, to help you decide which platform (or combination of platforms) best fits your goals.

UPLOADING YOUR BOOK

Uploading your book to these platforms requires preparation, patience, and a little bit of grace for yourself, because no matter how tech-savvy you are, something will likely confuse you the first time. It is not hard once the process is understood. Without that understanding, though, the on-screen steps can quickly feel frustrating and even daunting. I'll provide you with some helpful information to help guide you through the initial process. And, if that doesn't help you, then check YouTube and the resources mentioned in this book.

After you've created your accounts and logged in, you'll need to navigate a series of steps, entering book details, uploading interior and cover files, selecting categories, pricing, and finally approving the proof. Here's what you should know about each platform to save yourself time (and headaches):

Amazon KDP

1. **Ease of Use:** Beginner-friendly and completely free. Amazon KDP walks you step by step through the upload process, making it ideal for first-time self-publishers.
2. **What to Watch For:** The previewer tool is accurate for spotting formatting errors, but sometimes page breaks or image placement may look different once printed. Always order a **proof copy** before approving your book for sale.
3. **File Flexibility:** Changes can be made anytime without extra fees, which is a significant advantage if you're still catching minor typos or adjusting formatting.

Self-Publishing Advice: Amazon KDP automatically converts your manuscript into Kindle and print-ready files, but you should still upload a properly formatted PDF or ePub to ensure quality.

IngramSpark

- **Professional Reach, Professional Demands:** This platform is built for wide distribution, bookstores, libraries, and global outlets, but it expects a polished, professional file.
- **Fees & Changes:** There isn't an upload fee, but updates or file changes after approval cost extra (typically $25 per revision after 60 days), so make sure your manuscript is final.
- **What to Watch For:** IngramSpark can take longer to process files, sometimes **up to two weeks for approval**, and changes are not instant like Amazon KDP.

Self-Publishing Advice: Check their template library for cover and interior specs before uploading, margins, bleed, and spine width must be exact, or your files will be rejected.

Draft2Digital

- **eBook Excellence:** D2D shines for eBook distribution, automatically formatting your manuscript into professional-looking ePub files and distributing to platforms Amazon doesn't reach (Apple Books, Kobo, Nook, Scribd).
- **Print Option:** They offer print-on-demand for free, but it's relatively newer and lacks the customization options of IngramSpark.
- **What to Watch For:** D2D takes longer to print and ship author copies, several weeks in some cases, so plan if you need copies for an event.

Self-Publishing Advice: Be patient. All three platforms require you to **double-check your files** before hitting publish. This is an extra layer of quality assurance that you'll appreciate over time.

What you see in the previewer isn't always precisely what prints. Also, these platforms don't "talk" to each other, if you're publishing on multiple platforms, you'll need to manually upload files and adjust them to fit each platform's unique specs.

If you're unsure whether your files are truly ready, **hire a professional formatter or invest time in learning how to use each platform's templates correctly**. Skipping this step will lead to delays, rejections, and possibly wasted money on re-upload fees.

GETTING PROOFS & AUTHOR COPIES

Proof copies, in my opinion, are the **bread and butter** of publishing because they give you a glimpse into what your reader will experience. I've spent countless hours reviewing author copies after writing my manuscript and designing my book covers. I will **never** recommend publishing a book without seeing a proof first.

Why? Because proofs and author copies allow you to catch errors before your readers ever see them, things like misplaced titles, misspelled words, and sizing issues.

They also let you compare finishes, such as matte versus gloss covers, and give you confidence that your final product meets the level of quality your readers deserve. **Never skip this step.** Next, let's look at how to order proofs and what to expect with delivery times.

Author copies become available for purchase after you've officially submitted your book to be published. In most cases, you can get them before the book goes live to the public. These are especially useful for pre-orders, workshops, trainings, book signings, or for ARC readers (if you're not sending PDFs). Both proof and author copies are charged at printing and shipping costs only, you're not paying retail, which is great for maximizing your royalties later.

For example, I often sell books directly through my website. Using author copies allows me to earn a higher royalty, but it also means I must manage shipping myself, and these sales don't count toward industry rankings or official book sales. That's the trade-off.

When I released the *Oakland Hills, Milwaukee Rivers: A Memoir of Survival, Identity, and Purpose* (Second Edition), author copies made it possible to send free advance reader copies to everyone who purchased the first edition within the first 30 days, my way of saying thank you for their support.

This small gesture generated early buzz and encouraged readers to leave reviews. It was a thoughtful, strategic move that cost me $150, since I was covering only the printing costs.

. When you're publishing, consider opportunities like that to make an impact on your audience, as it may help you with future projects.

Below is what you can expect from each major distributor when it comes to proofs and author copies:

Amazon KDP

- Affordable and easy to order directly through your Amazon KDP dashboard.
- **Proof copies** have a large "Not for Resale" stripe on the cover, discouraging resale.
- **Damaged author copies:** Occasionally, books arrive with printing flaws. Amazon requires photos and proof before issuing refunds, so inspect every copy carefully before shipping to customers.

IngramSpark

- Known for **professional print quality** and wider trim-size options, but author copies are more expensive than Amazon's.
- Shipping times can take significantly longer (sometimes weeks).
- **Important:** Make all your decisions about paper and print during the proofing stage. If you decide to change your book's paper type or format (for example, black-and-white to color) **after 60 days**, IngramSpark will charge change fees, and in some cases, you'll need to upload files again and assign a new ISBN.

Draft2Digital

- Print author copies are available, but their system is newer, and turnaround times can be inconsistent.

- eBooks remain D2D's strength, so print author copies are better for small quantities or if you're primarily focused on eBook distribution.

Self-Publishing Advice: Inspect Every Copy! I learned this lesson the hard way. One year, I ordered a large volume of one of my books. While preparing to send copies to a customer, I noticed that 10 of them had smeared ink inside. I spent over an hour on the phone with Amazon KDP, sending photos and order confirmations before they finally confirmed my reimbursement.

Check every single copy before selling it. Please don't assume that because it came from the printer, it's perfect. Also, compare different paper options during the proof stage, some paper types look and feel better. Changing your paper type later can be costly, especially on IngramSpark, where changes after 60 days may require new files, new fees, and even a new ISBN.

CUSTOMER SERVICE: WHAT YOU SHOULD EXPECT

I shared earlier about my experience calling Amazon KDP over smeared author copies, but that wasn't the only time I've reached out for help. I've also used their chat feature, and let me be honest, that is one of Amazon's strengths. Having quick access to someone who can at least point you in the right direction is valuable when you're in the thick of trying to solve a problem.

However, **not all self-publishing platforms are created equal** when it comes to customer service, a common frustration discussed by YouTubers and authors across the internet.

What happens when you can't figure out how to do something, or worse, something goes wrong? How long will it take to fix? Are you talking to a real person, or sending messages into a void and waiting days for someone to reply?

The truth is, your ability to resolve problems directly impacts your ability to produce a high-quality book. I've had moments of "I can't believe this happened!" frustration, times when a small mistake delayed my launch simply because I couldn't get a timely response.

To be fair, not all the blame belongs to the companies. Sometimes, we make mistakes out of impatience or by not following directions carefully. I've been guilty of this more than once. Still, knowing **what to expect** can save you headaches.

Amazon KDP

- **Contact Methods:** Email, live chat, and request-a-callback (phone). Chat is the fastest option.
- **Responsiveness:** Fastest of the three, with email and chat support. Some authors have even been able to request callbacks.
- **Quality of Support:** Helpful for basic questions, but support is heavily scripted. If you have a technical or unusual issue, answers sometimes vary depending on the agent.
- **What Authors Say Online:** Many praise Amazon's quick responses, but some complain about repetitive copy-paste answers that don't fully resolve complex issues.

IngramSpark

- **Contact Methods: Email only** through their portal. No phone or chat support.
- **Responsiveness:** Slowest of the three, often taking **3–7 business days** to reply due to high demand.

- **Quality of Support:** Once you get a response, the staff are knowledgeable and professional, especially regarding industry standards.
- **What Authors Say Online:** Authors frequently express frustration with long wait times, especially when an urgent fix is needed for a launch.

Draft2Digital

- **Contact Methods:** Email only, but replies are fast and personal. No chat or phone option.
- **Responsiveness:** Known as one of the most responsive in the industry, with email replies often within **24 hours** and a friendly, personal tone.
- **Quality of Support:** Consistently rated as helpful and approachable, especially for eBook distribution questions.
- **What Authors Say Online:** Many self-publishers rave about D2D's customer service, describing it as "friendly," "human," and "reassuring," which can be a relief if you're new to publishing.

Self-Publishing Advice: Document Everything. Always record customer service interactions. When I contacted Amazon KDP about smeared author copies, I had to submit photos, purchase confirmations, and order details. It took over an hour on the phone and multiple follow-ups to get reimbursed.

Keep a record of every interaction, save emails, take screenshots, and write down the names of the agents you speak with. This will save you time and frustration if you need to escalate an issue. And one more thing: be patient and polite. The nicer you are, the more likely they'll go the extra mile for you.

In this book's Resources section, you'll find a "Customer Service At-a-Glance" guide with contact details for three publishing companies. It's helpful to have everything in one place for quick answers.

AUDIENCE REACH

I've talked a lot about these platforms already, thank goodness I'm only covering three, right? If I tried to break down every single option out there, this book would be the size of an encyclopedia, and neither of us has time for that. But audience reach is important enough to pause for a moment and discuss in detail.

When uploading your book, you'll choose distribution options. Many authors select all markets for maximum visibility, but not everyone needs global reach. Strategy can be better than wide distribution. Understand what you're signing up for. Here's what to expect from these platforms.

Amazon KDP

Amazon dominates the U.S. and international eBook and paperback markets, so if you want instant global access, this is the platform. Here's the catch: many bookstores and libraries avoid Amazon titles because they see it as a competitor. While you'll reach readers online worldwide, your book may never sit on the shelves of your favorite local bookstore if Amazon is your only distributor.

IngramSpark

Think of this as your golden ticket for bookstores and libraries. IngramSpark has long-standing relationships with retailers, which is why it's the standard for authors who want their book stocked in places like Barnes & Noble or ordered through library systems. If you're serious about traditional retail visibility, this is the platform to prioritize. Here's the drawback: costs are higher, and their shipping is slower than the other distributors.

Draft2Digital

D2D is a leading eBook platform. It gets your digital book onto platforms like Apple Books, Kobo, and Barnes & Noble Nook, which means you're reaching readers who may never browse Amazon. There is a challenge: Its print network is expanding, but it's not yet as large or established as IngramSpark. If you're primarily focused on reaching digital-first readers outside Amazon, this is your best option.

Self-Publishing Advice: To maximize distribution and reach, layer your publishing platforms strategically by not duplicating services unnecessarily. You'll discover some platforms are better for specific services and features.

For example, use Amazon KDP for Amazon sales, IngramSpark for bookstore and library reach, and D2D for eBook expansion into non-Amazon markets. Double-check your global rights and territories when setting up your book, and don't be afraid to start small and expand later.

BOOK TEMPLATES: RESPECTING THEIR POWER

While this may not sound like a traditional "service experience," it's a crucial part of the process. If your book isn't formatted correctly, you'll be stuck in a never-ending cycle of errors and delays. Trust me, nothing will give you publishing nightmares faster than seeing that dreaded *Your file has errors and cannot be processed* message after uploading.

Each of the platforms provides templates to help you get your book formatted correctly, but here's the reality: if you're doing this yourself and don't have design experience, you might find yourself going a little crazy. There's no greater frustration (sarcasm intended) than spending hours designing your book cover in Canva or Photoshop, only to upload it and receive a long list of fixes. They get an A+ for quality control, but that means you, the self-publishing author, will need to pay attention to every single detail before you can move forward.

In my chapter on book covers, I didn't dive deep into the nuances of trim sizes, staying within the print lines, or how page count affects your final cover dimensions. But here's what you need to know: the templates they provide are tied directly to your book's final page count. For example, if your page count changes, even by a few pages, you'll need a new template because the spine width changes. Some templates even round up page counts automatically, which can throw off your design if you're not paying attention.

And yes, this applies whether you design the cover yourself or hire a professional. I've been fortunate to work with skilled designers, but even then, I've had delays lasting days because an error had to be corrected before the book could move forward. Those delays can completely derail your timeline, especially if you're pushing toward a specific launch date.

PLATFORM INSIGHTS: BOOK TEMPLATES & DESIGN NUANCES

Amazon KDP

Offers downloadable templates for both paperback and hardcover, based on your trim size and page count. Beginner-friendly, but the system will reject your file if anything is even slightly outside the margins. Expect immediate error notifications after upload, which is good for catching mistakes but frustrating when you're making multiple revisions.

IngramSpark

Provides precise, print-industry-standard templates that must be followed exactly. Professional-quality results, but far less forgiving if you get it wrong. If you make a mistake, expect delays because you'll have to re-upload and possibly wait days for approval.

Draft2Digital

For print, its template system is newer and less customizable than Amazon or IngramSpark. Great for eBooks (automated formatting tools help clean up files). But print templates can feel a little limited if you want specific trim sizes.

Self-Publishing Advice: Inspect every detail before uploading. Double-check your page count, trim size, and spine width before downloading templates, and avoid last-minute content changes after designing your cover.

If you change your page count (even one page), you'll need to start over with new specs, no exceptions. For hardcover designs, be especially mindful of jacket flaps (IngramSpark) or bleed areas (Amazon KDP). Rushing this step can cost you days, or even weeks, of delays.

WHICH PLATFORM SHOULD YOU CHOOSE?

Now that we've explored the key factors to consider when choosing publishing distributors, it's natural to feel a bit overwhelmed. And rightfully so, there is a lot to decide on. This is why self-publishing isn't for the faint of heart. While it continues to grow because of its flexibility compared to traditional publishing, one truth remains: quality must always be at the forefront of your mind.

The magical question still lingers: "Which platform should you choose?" Honestly, it depends. Each of the three platforms I've discussed has unique benefits and challenges, which makes it hard to say there's a single "best" option. And remember, there are even more platforms out there, Lulu and Barnes & Noble Press, for example.

The key is to stay focused on what you're trying to accomplish with your publishing journey. Your goals will guide you to the right decision.

Here's my recommendation, based on experience:

- **If you're starting out:** Start with **Amazon KDP** for its simplicity, affordability, and beginner-friendly process.
- **If you want bookstore and library placement:** Use **IngramSpark** for its professional print distribution network.

If you want to expand your eBook reach beyond Amazon: Add D2D to your strategy, it's excellent for reaching platforms like Apple Books, Kobo, and Nook.

KEEPING IT SIMPLE VS. GOING WIDE

In the publishing industry, a **hardcover book with a jacketed cover (dust jacket)** is often considered the most prestigious format.

It's a standard many use to gauge the quality you're delivering to your customers. But not all distribution platforms offer this.

When I published my leadership book, I found that Amazon KDP and D2D offer hardcover options but not jacketed ones. IngramSpark provides jacketed hardcovers with excellent quality, but their customer service and turnaround times are slower, sometimes taking weeks to receive proof copies or over a month for author copies.

The smart approach many self-publishers do is to use all three platforms strategically, Amazon KDP for Amazon sales, IngramSpark for wide print distribution, and D2D for global eBook exposure. But it depends on what you're publishing. For example, if you're publishing a coloring book, you wouldn't put that in an eBook; therefore, D2D wouldn't be a contender. You'll need to make the best-informed choice for your specific needs.

PUBLISHING REFLECTION

At this stage, every decision you make, where you publish, how you price, and the quality you deliver, cements your reputation as an author.

The publishing world may not always feel fair, but readers don't care about excuses, they care about excellence.

Let your work prove what you already know: that your voice, your story, and your message belong on those shelves right alongside the bestsellers. Long after the marketing fades and the launch hype is over, your book will remain as a piece of your legacy.

Make sure it's one you'll be proud to have speak for you, today, tomorrow, and for generations to come.

CHAPTER 13
BOOK PRICING
& PROFITABILITY

IT IS ESSENTIAL TO UNDERSTAND the full operational elements of using publishing platforms, but mastering them takes time and patience. As more resources are created to support self-publishing authors, this chapter focuses on pricing. Its purpose is to give a clear picture of what to expect.

Pricing is a strategy. The price you set can determine how competitive your book is, how readers perceive its quality, and ultimately how many units you sell. Before finalizing your price, research what similar books in your genre are selling for, especially on platforms like Amazon KDP. If comparable memoirs or self-help books are priced between $12.99 and $17.99, and you set yours at $24.99, you risk turning readers away.

Conversely, pricing too low can make your work seem less credible. In this chapter, we'll explore strategies for setting prices, understanding royalty structures, and balancing profitability with accessibility

I want to share a quick pricing example with you. I recently compared two self-published memoirs in the same category on Amazon, one priced at $14.99 and another at $21.99. The $14.99 book had over 500 reviews and ranked higher in sales, while the $21.99 book had fewer than 50 reviews and struggled to gain traction. The difference here was that readers saw the first book as reasonably priced for the value. The higher-priced book may have been good, but the higher price discouraged impulse buys.

A little research goes a long way: study your competitors, consider your print costs, and aim for a balance between affordability and perceived value.

- **Amazon KDP eBooks:** 70% royalty (if priced $2.99–$9.99).
- **Amazon Print:** Around 60% royalty minus printing costs.
- **IngramSpark Print:** 45–55% wholesale discount recommended for bookstores (they won't order your book without a discount).

PRICING YOUR BOOK STRATEGICALLY

A common mistake new self-publishing authors make is setting a price based on how much they think their book is worth instead of what the market will bear. Yes, the book may feel priceless, it holds your blood, sweat, and tears bound in pages. However, readers do not buy based on effort. They buy based on value and the quality they perceive compared to other books in the genre.

This is where **market research** becomes critical. If you set your price too high compared to similar books, you risk losing readers to competitors. If you set it too low, you may devalue your work and miss out on profit.

As a resource to help you determine your price, you have access to a "Book Pricing Strategy Worksheet" in the Resources section. This resource is a structured tool, often a one-page chart or table, that helps self-publishing authors set the best price for a book. It walks through key factors such as genre, length, and market demand that influence pricing. It forces you to *think like a businessperson* rather than guessing a random price.

In preparation for pricing your book, follow the steps below to guide you in making a decision, or utilize the actual worksheet that is provided.

Here is what you should do to get started with this process:

- **Research Comparable Titles on Amazon KDP and Other Platforms**
    - Search for books in your exact genre and category, memoirs, self-help, leadership, etc.
    - Pay attention to *page count, format* (paperback vs. hardcover), and *author experience* when comparing.
    - Look at the pricing sweet spot: for example, most paperback memoirs under 250 pages sell between **$12.99–$17.99**, while eBooks typically range **$3.99–$9.99**.
- **Consider the Psychology of Pricing**
    - Prices ending in *.99* often convert better because they feel lower to the buyer.
    - Avoid pricing too high (like $19.99+) unless you're targeting a niche or premium audience that expects it.
- **Start Competitively, Then Adjust**
    - New self-publishing authors should set their price below competitors' mid-range to attract early buyers. After gathering reviews and momentum, they can increase the price.
- **Balance Affordability With Profitability**
    - Don't underprice to make sales: If your book costs $6.00 to print and you price it at $8.99, you'll have almost no margin left after platform royalties and print costs.
    - Aim for a price that respects your work, covers your costs, and still feels reasonable to readers in your category.

With these three factors, research, psychology, and balance, you can set a price that benefits both your readers and your bottom line. Next, we'll explore specific pricing tactics to position your book for sales and sustainability.

- **Factor in Print Costs and Royalties**
  - Platforms like Amazon KDP have calculators showing print costs and royalties. If printing costs $5.00 and you price it at $9.99, the profit is slim. Avoid pricing too low for tiny profit or too high to deter buyers.
- **Think Long-Term, Not Just Launch**
  - If your goal is to attract speaking gigs, coaching clients, or build credibility, treat your book as marketing, not profit. Consider lower prices to sell more copies.

Pricing is critical to your publishing strategy, so take time to explore what works best for your book. It's better to price low, generate sales, and increase your chances of reviews than to set a high price and have no sales at all. This applies especially for new authors or initial launches.

LESSON LEARNED: DISTRIBUTION IS A LONG GAME

At the beginning of my publishing journey, I thought Amazon was all I needed. But when people started asking, "Can I get it at Barnes & Noble?" I had to scramble to find other distribution platforms, eventually uploading my book to IngramSpark. This delay cost me potential sales and visibility.

Now, every time I release a book, I plan distribution **before** launch day. This means:

- Buying my ISBNs early.
- Uploading to both Amazon KDP and IngramSpark before the official release date.
- Making sure my metadata is consistent across platforms.

In summary, each platform offers unique advantages, and the best choice depends on your publishing goals.

- Amazon KDP gives you unmatched reach and convenience, making it ideal for first-time self-publishing authors, but its exclusivity options (like Amazon KDP Select) can limit your distribution.
- IngramSpark is perfect for wide distribution and bookstore placement, giving your book a professional edge, though it requires upfront costs and a learning curve.
- D2D is a strong alternative for those wanting wide eBook distribution with user-friendly tools, but it's primarily digital-focused.

The sooner you plan distribution, the fewer surprises you'll face on launch day, and the smoother your sales journey will be.

Many successful self-publishing authors, including me, use a combination of these platforms to maximize both reach and revenue.

The key is to understand your goals, whether it's selling everywhere, looking professional in bookstores, or keeping things simple, and choose the mix that works for you. You may find that you want to use only one because of the complexity of navigating multiple systems. And that is alright.

As a self-publishing author running a small press, I sometimes find it challenging to navigate all the systems required to stay competitive and visible. In the end, the right distribution mix isn't about doing it all, it's about choosing what makes sense for your book, your readers, and your long-term goals.

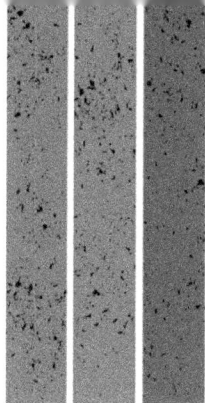

CHAPTER 14
PREPARING FOR LAUNCH

"This is my story, my legacy, and my contribution to the world."

SAY THIS TO YOURSELF NOW, because soon, the world will finally hold what you've poured your time, energy, and heart into.

THE REALITY OF THIS MOMENT

You've made it. Your manuscript is written, edited, polished, formatted, and uploaded. The cover looks professional. The ISBN, copyright, and metadata are all in place. You've officially hit that "Publish" button.

Now, you wait.

This waiting period feels different. It's not only technical but also emotional. This is where you, as a self-publishing author, must face the truth that your work is about to live in the hands of readers who will have opinions, questions, and, yes, sometimes criticism.

For Black authors especially, this moment carries an added weight. We do not always get the grace of trial and error. Our books are often judged not only on content but also on whether they meet or exceed industry standards. This comes from a long history of systemic bias in publishing, where our stories have too often been overlooked, undervalued, or confined to the spaces where we coexist. This is why excellence matters even more; we are not only representing ourselves but also opening doors for others who will follow.

But here's the beautiful part: your story has power. You wrote it for a reason. You chose to put your name on that cover for a reason. And now, as nerve-wracking as this feels, you're about to step into a new identity, author.

SALES AND YOUR INTEGRITY

Before we move into the marketing phase, I want to slow you down for a moment. This is where your integrity as an author is validated—where you confirm that you're proud of what you've created, not because it's done, but because it reflects your professionalism and your story. I know how nerve-wracking this can feel.

It's tempting to rush ahead to the excitement of sales and promotion, but pausing here ensures you're not selling a product—you're standing behind something you believe in. Integrity in publishing means you can look your readers in the eye, knowing you've done your best. Your confidence becomes the foundation for every marketing strategy you use later.

You're probably asking yourself:

- *What will people think about what I've written?*
- *Am I ready for the questions they might ask about my story?*
- *Did I do everything I could to make this book the best it could be?*

I've said similar things in all my books, as they often reveal vulnerable parts of my life. Yet, I always had to remember it was my story, my truth, my decision. Now, I remind you: your story is yours and worth telling. Center yourself in that truth before the world responds.

Because I want you to have something tangible, I thought carefully about my process and identified 10 things I could include in this book to leave with you as useful tools and resources. They are listed below for you.

TOP 10 THINGS TO HAVE READY BEFORE LAUNCH DAY

This isn't just a checklist; it's a commitment to professionalism and confidence. Treat this like your final pre-launch inspection before the world sees your work, because once they see it, they can't unsee it.

I've done my best to inform you to take your time and get things aligned so that when you get to this point, you'll be ready. If you've followed the advice, you'll be well-prepared. No pressure, just confidence. Think of this as your quality control step, the safeguard that protects you from small mistakes that can make a big impact. Do it carefully, and you'll release your book with the kind of confidence that shows in every detail.

1. A Final Proofed Copy for Peace of Mind

Read your final proof as if you're the customer. Would you be proud to hand this to someone? Even if you've edited it a hundred times, hold it, flip through it, and ask yourself that question.

You never get a second chance to make a first impression. Your writing is your intellectual property, protect it. If you used a professional editor or formatter, keep the final Word and PDF copies. This way, if future changes are needed, you'll have the source document to prevent you from starting from scratch.

2. ISBNs Purchased and Assigned

Own your publishing identity. Don't rely solely on free ISBNs from Amazon KDP. Purchase your own through Bowker (U.S.) or the equivalent in your country to maintain full control and broader distribution. This ensures that your book is tied to you or your imprint and not a platform.

3. A Professional Cover (Correctly Sized for Each Platform)

Your cover is your first salesperson. Make sure it's sized to the specs for both Amazon KDP and IngramSpark if you're using both. Pay close attention to spine width, bleed, and trim sizes. A cover that doesn't fit perfectly will scream "self-published," and since it's the first thing a person sees when shopping for a book, you don't want yours to be the one they skip.

4. Metadata Finalized and Consistent

Your book must be findable. This includes your title, subtitle, author name, categories, keywords, and description. Keep it consistent across every platform to avoid confusion in search engines and catalogs.

5. Pricing Strategy Locked In

Price with intention, not emotion. Research comparable titles in your genre, balance affordability with profitability, and set your price accordingly. Decide on discounts for IngramSpark (bookstores expect them) and make sure your eBook price aligns with reader expectations.

6. Marketing Materials Prepared

Don't wait until launch week to scramble. Have your graphics, social posts, and email announcements drafted ahead of time. This allows you to focus on engaging with readers during your launch instead of creating content at the last minute.

7. Advance Readers and Early Reviews

Leverage feedback and build buzz. Get your book into the hands of beta readers, ARC readers, or trusted supporters ahead of launch. Their early reviews can help you start strong and give potential buyers confidence in your work.

8. Distribution Accounts Ready (Amazon KDP, IngramSpark, D2D, etc.)

Avoid last-minute setup headaches. Create and test your publishing accounts early, complete tax and payment details, and familiarize yourself with each platform's quirks. Don't wait until launch week to discover issues.

9. Proof Copies or Author Copies Ordered

See it the way your reader will. Holding the physical book reveals issues digital files can't, color differences, font sizes, margins, or cover alignment. Always order and review a proof copy before giving your final approval.

10. A Launch Day Checklist (and Backup Plan)

Plan for success, prepare for surprises. Write out what you'll do on launch day: announce on social, send your email newsletter, and celebrate with your supporters. At the same time, have a backup plan in case something goes wrong (like a delayed upload). Flexibility reduces stress.

These ten steps represent the foundation of a strong, confident launch. Each one moves you from uncertainty to readiness by covering many of the essential details you'll need to be effective. This is from ISBNs to your launch-day strategy. If you complete them all, you'll be prepared and position yourself as a professional author ready to release your work into the world.

CELEBRATE THIS ACCOMPLISHMENT

The night before launch, hold your book or proof copy and say aloud, "This is my story, my legacy, and my contribution to the world." It may feel corny, but the confidence it builds matters. Preparation is only half the journey. Once your book is ready, the real challenge begins: making sure readers can find it. This is where your visibility plan comes in.

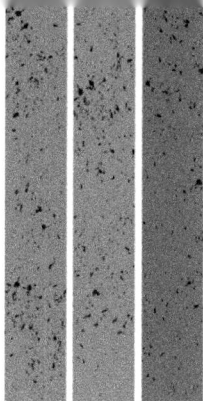

CHAPTER 15
THE VISIBILITY PLAN

WHEN I STEPPED INTO SELF-PUBLISHING, I didn't know about the mechanisms behind the platforms that decide how, when, and if your book is ever found online. It felt like a different language, something from another planet, a complete mystery.

I quickly learned that you could create a stunning cover, craft the perfect back cover blurb, and still miss out on readers if you don't understand how discoverability works online. In a bookstore, your book has a chance to catch someone's eye when they pick it up and flip it over. Online, you don't get that luxury. You only have about one to eight seconds to convince a potential buyer that your book is exactly what they've been searching for. This short timeframe can be the make-or-break moment for your sales.

How do you do that? How do you make sure your book appeals not only to readers, but to Google and Amazon's search engines? How do you capture attention before someone scrolls past? And how do you ensure your book shows up in search results at all?

These are the questions I had to wrestle with, and honestly, ones I'm still learning about every day.

The world of self-publishing is always evolving. But what I want to share with you here are the insights I've gathered through trial, error, and persistence. Consider this a compilation of insights from my journey, designed to help you avoid the pitfalls I encountered.

In this chapter, we're going to dive into the three behind-the-scenes elements that make or break your book's discoverability:

- **Keywords**: The search terms that connect your book to the right readers.
- **Categories**: Your online "shelves" that determine where your book lives and how competitive it is.
- **Product Descriptions**: This is your book's digital sales pitch that works differently from your back cover blurb.

By the time we're done, you'll know not only how these pieces work, but also how to use them strategically, sometimes even with the help of AI, to make your book visible, appealing, and primed for sales.

KEYWORDS: THE LANGUAGE OF SEARCH

At the beginning of this book, I introduced you to KeyWORDS, the motivational quotes that I used to post on Facebook. Now, I'd like to discuss keywords, the crucial connection point between your book and readers searching online.

Two impactful terms, with two different outcomes.

Keywords are the terms that connect your book to the right readers. Think about when you go online to find your favorite romance novel, a leadership book that provides practical tools to solve a problem, or a self-help book to guide you through a new journey. You don't just type "book" into the search bar. You use specific words and phrases that describe exactly what you're looking for.

That's the structure keywords give.

You should think about it from this perspective: **your keywords are the bridge between a reader's problem and your book as their solution.**

WHY KEYWORDS MATTER

There are three specific things that we need to focus on: visibility, connection, and sales impact. These three components contribute to your book's discoverability.

It doesn't matter how powerful your book is if no one can find it. The wrong keywords (or worse, no keywords at all) can bury your book so deep in search results that it never gets discovered. But the right keywords act like a spotlight, pulling your book forward in the exact moment a reader is looking for help, inspiration, or a good story.

Think about it like this:

- **Visibility:** Keywords help your book show up in searches when readers don't even know your name yet.
- **Connection:** They introduce your book to the reader who's saying, *I need this in my life*.
- **Momentum:** On Amazon and Google, keywords directly influence your rankings, your discoverability, and even your chance to land on bestseller lists.

When you step back and look at these three areas, visibility, connection, and momentum, it becomes clear that keywords are not just an afterthought, but they're also the foundation of how your book gets discovered. They shape whether your book sits buried under thousands of others or rises to meet the exact reader who needs it. And the best part is, keywords aren't random, they're strategic. Once you understand the types of keywords available to you and how to use them, you'll have a powerful advantage in positioning your book for success.

THE TWO KINDS OF KEYWORDS

Keywords come in two different forms: general and long-tail. Depending on your book and its genre, you may need to diversify your strategy to increase searchability.

- **General Keywords:** These are broad terms like leadership, faith, romance, and motivation. They get a lot of traffic, but they're also highly competitive. Imagine standing in a crowded room trying to get someone's attention, it's possible, but it's tough.
- **Long-Tail Keywords:** These are specific phrases like a Christian leadership book for new managers or a memoir about healing after parent loss. They may not get as much traffic, but when someone types in a long-tail keyword, they're not browsing, they're ready. They're saying, "I want exactly this." If your book fits, you've found your ideal reader.

Understanding the difference between general and long-tail keywords is only the first step. The real power comes in knowing how to discover the right ones for your specific book and audience. In the next section, we'll walk through practical strategies and tools you can use to uncover keywords that give your book the best chance of being found.

HOW TO DISCOVER THE RIGHT KEYWORDS

When I first encountered the term 'keywords' and understood their importance for books, my immediate question was, "How do I find the right ones?" I'm sure you share this question, as it's not easily answered. The strategy is simple: act like a customer. Since your book aims to solve a problem, observe what happens when you search for solutions.

Start with Amazon's Search Bar

Amazon is the world's largest bookstore, so millions of people are going online each day looking for things. Type in one word connected to your book and see what auto-suggestions pop up. Those suggestions are gold, they're what people are typing in right now. Write them down to use for your keywords.

Utilize Tools

There are tools like Google Trends or Keyword Planner to assist you. These tools can help you see how often certain terms are searched. It's like a window into the mind of your potential reader. Or, if you're ready to invest, tools like Publisher Rocket or Helium 10 can save you hours of guesswork by showing you exactly what readers are searching for, and how competitive those terms are.

Study Your Competitors

One strategy that I've started doing is reviewing books within the genre I plan to publish in. Books like yours provide valuable insights. Identify the words that consistently appear in subtitles, descriptions, or reviews. Those are your clues.

Remember, self-publishing isn't an easy process, but there are ways to succeed. I recommend working more efficiently, so I want to share a secret with you: Artificial Intelligence. Yes, I said it. Artificial Intelligence can be a helpful tool, and I'll give some ideas in this chapter on how to use it to your advantage.

To ensure you gather useful information from this chapter, I invite you to participate in an exercise that is also listed in the Resources section of this book. This exercise may feel small, but it's one of the most important steps you'll take in giving your book a real chance to be seen. I've created a space for you below to do this.

Completing the exercise below will significantly support your later processes.

EXERCISE 1: DISCOVERING KEYWORDS

1. Write down 10 words or phrases you believe your target reader would type into Amazon or Google to find your book.
2. Circle the ones that are most specific to your message or story.
3. Choose 5 that best capture the bridge between the reader's problem and your book as the solution.

_____

_____

_____

_____

_____

_____

_____

_____

_____

_____

_____

LET ARTIFICIAL INTELLIGENCE (AI) HELP YOU

Artificial Intelligence can be a powerful ally in self-publishing. It is a tool that can save you time, so make use of it. I, too, felt overwhelmed trying to understand and master all the nuances of self-publishing, and as a result, I sought ways to save time, money, and my sanity. AI was one of those ways. If this feels overwhelming or you want a head start, you can use AI tools like ChatGPT to generate keyword lists for you.

Here's a prompt you can use after uploading your manuscript to the AI platform, ChatGPT:

Based on my attached manuscript, generate a list of 15 highly relevant keywords and long-tail phrases optimized for Amazon and Google searches. Focus on terms my target readers are most likely to type when looking for a book like mine.

After doing this, use what you have as a starting point, not the finish line. Read through the list. During your process, ask yourself: *Do these words sound like something my reader would type? Do they fit my book naturally?* If so, embrace it as a resource to reduce the stress of self-publishing.

Remember, AI can give you suggestions, but only you know your story and your audience well enough to choose the ones that truly resonate.

Here is a publishing tip: AI can help study competitors and identify relevant keywords. Here is how to approach it:

1. Review five of your competitors' descriptions and put them into a Word document.
2. Ask ChatGPT to provide a list of the common keywords used within those descriptions.
3. Identify common words and incorporate them into your list.

This strategy will help you understand what to include in the necessary descriptions, while also gathering useful keywords to enhance your SEO fields on the platform.

Keywords go beyond data; they form the invisible bridge that connects readers to your message. Treat them like an extension of your story. Because when the right person types the right phrase and finds your book, that's not a sale—it's a connection.

CATEGORIES: WHERE YOUR BOOK LIVES

If keywords are the invisible strings that connect readers to your book, categories are the shelves that tell the world where your book belongs.

Think about walking into a bookstore. You don't see books tossed around. They're organized into sections: Fiction, Nonfiction, Leadership, Romance, Self-Help, Memoir, Spiritual Growth, the list goes on. These categories guide the reader's journey. If they're looking for a new romance novel, they don't go to the Business section. If they want a book on leadership, they don't wander into Poetry. Categories matter.

Now take that same concept and move it online. On Amazon, Barnes & Noble, IngramSpark, and other platforms, categories do the same thing, they tell the system where to place your book and tell readers where to find it.

Here's the part most new authors don't realize: your category choice doesn't just affect where your book shows up; it also affects whether you ever hit a bestseller list. It all works together to identify the message that you wrote to share with the world.

WHY CATEGORIES MATTER

You may be wondering, "Why do categories matter so much?" And because that's a common question, it's important to explain. There are four primary reasons to be aware of: visibility, competition, credibility, and momentum.

Let's take a moment to break them down for clarity.

- **Visibility:** Categories are like doors. Choose the wrong one, and your book might be hidden behind doors no one ever opens. Choose the right one, and your book sits on a shelf where people are actively browsing.
- **Competition:** Some categories are so crowded that new books get swallowed up. Others are smaller and offer a real chance to stand out.
- **Credibility:** Being listed in the right category signals to readers, "Yes, this book is exactly what you're looking for."
- **Momentum:** On Amazon, if you sell enough books in your chosen category, even in a short burst, you can earn a "#1 Bestseller" tag. And that badge is a magnet for buyers.

UNDERSTANDING CATEGORIES

There are two main types you need to know about:

1. **BISAC Codes:** These are the standard book industry categories (used by libraries, bookstores, and IngramSpark). Think of them as the official map. You'll select at least one BISAC code when you set up your book.
2. **Amazon Categories:** Amazon takes BISAC codes and breaks them down into more detailed subcategories. This is where strategy comes in. For example:
   a. BISAC: SELF-HELP / Personal Growth
   b. Amazon Subcategories: Self-Help > Personal Growth > Motivation & Inspiration OR Self-Help > Personal Growth > Spiritual.

On Amazon, you typically get to choose two main categories at setup, but you can request to be added to more later. That's a secret many authors don't know. They think they're stuck with just two, but you can expand your reach by asking Amazon to add your book to additional subcategories.

HOW TO CHOOSE THE RIGHT CATEGORIES

Here's a simple strategy I've used and taught:

- **Look at Similar Books:** Go to Amazon and find books like yours. Scroll down to the product details and see which categories they're listed in. Write them down.
- **Check the Competition:** How many books are in that category? If there are 50, 000+ books, it's going to be hard to rank. But if you find a subcategory with a few thousand, your chances improve dramatically.
- **Balance Broad and Niche:** A broad category gives you exposure but lots of competition. A niche category may have less traffic, but it positions your book to rank and potentially earn a bestseller badge.
- **Choose Two for Launch:** Pick one broad category and one niche category. This way, you get the best of both worlds.

To provide you with a practical tool and strategy for your publishing journey, I would like to invite you again to do an exercise that will be useful in the future, whether you publish your first book or later ones. It has been invaluable to me, and I do it when working on my own publications or those of a client.

EXERCISE 2

Pick a few books at home or search online for books that are like yours, those in the same genre, tone, or subject. Look them up on Amazon and see what categories they fall into.

Ask yourself these questions:

Do these categories also fit my book?
Which ones feel too crowded?

Which ones give me room to stand out?

Circle the two that feel like the best fit for your launch. Write down two alternates you may want to request later.

EXERCISE 2: SELECTING CATEGORIES

1. _____

2. _____

3. _____

4. _____

5. _____

6. _____

7. _____

LEVERAGE ARTIFICIAL INTELLIGENCE (AI) FOR YOUR WORK

As with keywords, AI can provide a valuable starting point when selecting categories. If you use ChatGPT, open it up, load your book manuscript, and use this prompt to assist you.

Here's a prompt you can use after uploading your manuscript:

Using my attached manuscript, recommend five Amazon book categories (and their corresponding subcategories) where my book would be competitive and discoverable. Provide a mix of broad and niche categories.

The list AI gives you isn't final, it's a starting point. Your job is to double-check and ensure that the categories accurately reflect your book's content and your goals. While you do that, also consider other books that are in the top 100 bestseller list that your book's genre would live in. Use AI as a tool to surface options quickly, but let your final decisions be guided by strategy, alignment, and real-world marketplace trends.

I want you to keep in mind that Categories aren't boxes to check. They are opportunities to position your book where it has the best chance to be found, to stand out, and to succeed. Choose wisely, and your book won't fade into the background—it will stand out on the right shelf.

PRODUCT DESCRIPTIONS: YOUR BOOK'S DIGITAL SALES PITCH

Your cover might catch someone's eye. Your title might spark their curiosity. But when it comes down to it, the product description is often the deciding factor between a reader buying your book or scrolling past it.

Think of the product description as your digital handshake. In a bookstore, a reader can pick up your book, feel its weight, flip through the pages, and read the back cover. Online, you don't get that luxury. The product description becomes the only place where you can directly speak to a reader and say, *Here's why this book is for you.*

And here's the part that trips up many new authors: your back cover blurb and your online product description are not the same thing. The blurb is emotional, it's about intrigue and curiosity. The product description, however, must balance both emotion and sales psychology. It's more than telling readers what your book is about—it's about showing them why it matters.

THE IMPACT OF PRODUCT DESCRIPTIONS

I'd hate to suggest that product descriptions don't matter, because the truth is, they're equally, if not more, important than your back cover blurb. But why? There are many reasons, but the main ones are first impressions, search engine optimization, and conversion ability. They are essential to your book's success, and I want to take a moment to explain this so you can achieve it.

- **First Impressions Count**: In a crowded marketplace, your description must capture attention within the first few lines.
- **Search-Friendly**: Keywords and phrases woven into your description help with search results.
- **Conversion Power**: A good description moves readers from interested to committed

How do you craft an effective product description? This is a valid question, and I recently discovered the answer, so I want to share it with you. Of course, you could sit down and write a compelling summary of your book without any tools or resources. However, in today's industry, having a strategy and a framework is essential. That's why I want to introduce you to the AIDA Framework.

THE AIDA FRAMEWORK

A simple and effective way to craft your product description is by using the AIDA model. It's a framework first introduced in 1898 by an American advertising pioneer named E. St. Elmo Lewis. He studied how salespeople could effectively guide potential customers from first noticing a product to ultimately making a purchase.

There are four stages of the model: (1) attention, (2) interest, (3) desire, and (4) action. It originally served as a sales tool for print advertising, such as magazine ads, newspaper promotions, and door-to-door sales pitches, and has become one of the most lasting marketing formulas in history.

Over the years, AIDA has been used in radio, TV, email marketing, and now digital platforms like Amazon product pages. Since it's such a powerful tool for creating product descriptions in book publishing, I wanted to include it in this chapter to give you an advantage in your publishing journey. I will explain more below.

The reason the AIDA framework stays effective is simple: human psychology hasn't changed.

As readers, we are easily distracted, that's where Attention comes into play. We still need compelling reasons to continue reading, that's Interest. We want to know what's in it for us, that's Desire. And we are more likely to respond when we're clearly told what to do next, that's Action. For authors, this model is powerful because it helps you avoid writing vague or dull product descriptions. Instead, it offers a proven structure that guides your words and creates copy that not only describes your book but also persuades someone to buy it.

In the text below, I offer a deeper insight into AIDA and how it can work for you as you consider developing your own product description.

Attention: Start with a compelling hook that grabs the reader's attention and makes them want to keep scrolling.
Example: "You have a story inside you, but the publishing world makes it harder than it should be."

Interest: Share some details that capture their attention.

Example: "Too many aspiring authors give up because publishing feels confusing, expensive, and full of hidden rules."

Desire: Show the transformation they will experience through your book.

Example: "With this guide, you won't only publish, you'll publish with clarity, confidence, and a plan for success."

Action: Encourage them to make a purchase.

Example: "Start your publishing journey today and get your book into the world."

Understanding the AIDA framework gives you the foundation for persuasive book marketing. Now let's take it a step further with practical writing tips you can apply right away to make your descriptions, ads, and posts even more compelling.

WRITING TIPS THAT SELL

When writing your product description, keep in mind the character limits. It's also important to remember that people's attention spans are short. Therefore, make it concise, aim for 150–200 words. Online shoppers tend to skim.

- **Break it up:** Use short paragraphs and even bullet points if the platform allows.
- **Use emotional + practical language:** Speak to both the heart ("your story deserves to be told") and the head ("step-by-step guidance from idea to launch").
- **End with urgency:** Give the reader a reason to act now, not later.

Try This Exercise

Spend five minutes drafting a product description for your book using the AIDA framework. Don't overthink it—write.

When you do this, you ask yourself the following questions:

What one sentence will grab Attention?
What quick detail builds Interest?
What transformation sparks Desire?
What call to Action invites them to buy?

Read it aloud. Does it sound like you? Does it make you want to pick up your own book? If it doesn't, then refine you're approach for multiple options until you're satisfied with the outcome.

USING ARTIFICIAL INTELLIGENCE (AI) FOR PRODUCT DESCRIPTIONS

If writing sales copy causes you to freeze up, AI can help you get started.

Here's a prompt you can use after uploading your manuscript to ChatGPT.

Using my manuscript (attached), write a compelling 200-word product description for Amazon using the AIDA formula (Attention, Interest, Desire, Action). Make it emotional, persuasive, and optimized for online book platforms.

Take the draft AI provides and refine it with your own voice because readers connect with authenticity. AI gives you the bones, but you bring the heartbeat.

Your product description isn't an afterthought, it's your sales pitch. When done effectively, it can persuade a reader from curiosity to commitment in under a minute. And when combined with the right keywords and categories, it becomes part of the engine that helps your book reach the readers who need it most.

BRINGING IT ALL TOGETHER

We've covered a lot in this chapter, keywords, categories, and product descriptions. Each one is powerful on its own, but together they create the engine of discoverability that helps your book not only exist online but also be found, seen, and purchased.

Here's the key takeaway: publishing a book is about positioning it for discoverability. The good news is that positioning isn't guesswork. By researching your keywords, carefully selecting categories, and writing a compelling product description, you're not checking boxes, you're opening doors for readers to find your message, your story, your wisdom.

And remember, none of these choices are permanent. You can always revisit your keywords, update your categories, and refresh your description as you learn more about your audience. That's the beauty of self-publishing. You get to adapt and grow alongside your readers.

Don't let this overwhelm you. Instead, treat it like planting seeds. Every choice you make here has the potential to reach someone who needs your book. With time, attention, and intention, those seeds grow into visibility, sales, and impact.

The power of discoverability lies in the details. By applying what you've learned, you're not only publishing, but you're also strategically positioning your book to reach the readers who need it most.

.

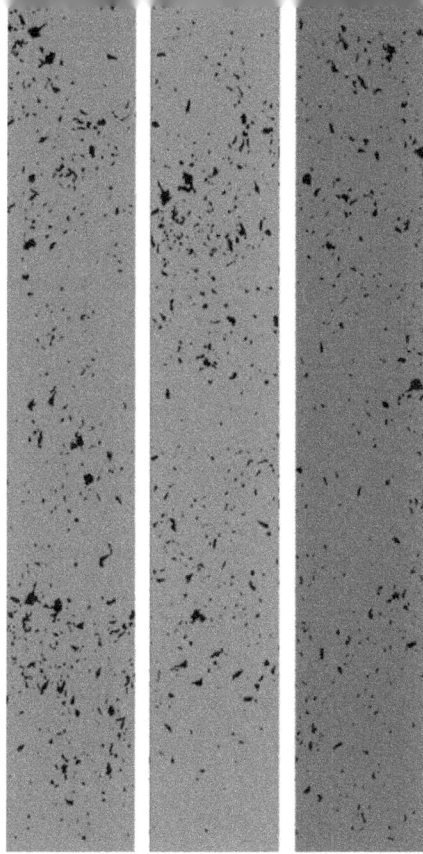

LAUNCH AND MARKETING

CHAPTER 16

BUILDING YOUR LAUNCH TEAM

I PROMISE TO TELL THE TRUTH, the whole truth, and nothing but the truth. Sound familiar? Good because I intend to be completely raw and honest. I'll start with this: I hate marketing. I truly dislike it. But I'll admit, it's become fascinating to study.

Why do I hate it? Because, as a self-publishing author, it can feel like I'm begging people to support me. And *that* part? I don't like at all.

During my first book, I thought my family and friends would be all I needed to get the word out. I posted on Facebook, texted people, and assumed everyone who said, "I can't wait to read it!" would buy the book and leave a review.

Ready for the truth? They didn't. A few read it, even fewer left reviews. Not because they didn't care, but because life is busy, and unless you guide people, they won't automatically invest in your success. I've learned that most people will only consistently support you if it directly benefits them. Now, that's not everyone, but it's a lot of people.

That was my first wake-up call as a self-publishing author: **you need a team, not cheerleaders.**

A book launch isn't about hitting "publish." It's about creating excitement, building anticipation, and making sure your book gets into the hands of the right people, fast. And that doesn't happen by accident. It occurs when you have a group of people intentionally supporting you before your book even releases.

In my case, I didn't have that team around me. Honestly, I might have talked about my book so much that I annoyed people. Even now, I try to be conscious about how much I talk about writing because, while it's my life, it's not everyone else's, and most people don't care as much as we think they do.

WHAT IS A LAUNCH TEAM?

Even if your closest friends don't help you get the word out, how do you do it? The answer: **a launch team.**

Think of a launch team as your personal group of advocates, the people who step in to do four critical things:

- Buy (or receive) your book early.
- Leave honest reviews as soon as they go live.
- Share your book with their networks, on social media, in conversations, or even in group chats.
- Give you moral support when impostor syndrome creeps in (and trust me, it will).

Your launch team doesn't need to be huge, 10–20 committed people can make a massive difference, but they need to be intentional and aligned with your book's purpose.

You're probably thinking, "*10–20 committed people?*" Yes, I'm serious. The more people you can recruit, the better. People usually act only after seeing or hearing something multiple times. That's when curiosity kicks in, and they finally ask, "What's this book about?"

But here's the hard part: getting those people and choosing the right ones. If you're not careful, you'll end up frustrated, wondering why you bothered to ask certain people in the first place. This is why you need to be strategic in selecting your launch team, and not filling spots with anyone who says yes.

WHO SHOULD BE ON YOUR LAUNCH TEAM?

Here's where I made a critical mistake: I originally invited anyone who said, "I'm proud of you!" or "I love to read" to be one of my launch team members, a significant error. You want people who will take action.

When I released my first publication, I shared it with Beta readers and asked for feedback. The feedback was positive, and since they weren't people I had a personal relationship with, it felt great to have unbiased opinions. One of those Beta readers eventually became close and wanted to help me with things that would increase my book's visibility. At first, I thought, *Great! This is exactly the kind of support I need.*

But here's the truth, he quickly proved otherwise. He offered advice and, at times, even tried to "direct" me as if he had a monopoly on book marketing. Still, I decided to give him a chance and test his follow-through.

I gave him a simple task: look up some information online and provide it to me within a specific timeframe. He did some work but turned in an incomplete list. **Strike one.** Later, he came back asking what else he could do to help. Again, I assigned him a task to gather some information and report back. Time passed. Nothing. **Strike two.**

Then, like clockwork, he popped up again, full of excitement, asking how he could support me. At that point, I was honest with him, I told him I don't like it when people don't keep their word. He apologized and promised he would do better. I gave him one final task: make a connection with some people in his circle who could help. Supposedly, some progress was made, but no real results or confirmation ever came. And when I saw the same patterns repeating? Strike three, you're out.

I ceased communication because I realized he was wasting my time, and time is something you cannot afford to waste when launching a book. I share this because **you need people who will support your vision and deliver on their promises.** If they can't, acknowledge it and disconnect them from the task.

Your book is too important to have people around you who won't produce results.

When selecting your team, look for:

- People in your target audience (or those who connect with your message).
- Influencers in their communities or online.
- Friends or colleagues who are reliable and follow through on commitments.
- Networks such as churches, professional circles, book clubs, and community groups.

The strength of your launch team depends on choosing people who care, commit, and carry through. Avoid filling it with people who *want to be nice* but won't leave honest, constructive reviews.

HOW TO RECRUIT YOUR LAUNCH TEAM

You might be nervous about asking people for help. I was, too, but remember, you're inviting them into something bigger than a book. You're asking them to help you change lives, and that is what you should focus on. This ties back to my earlier point about knowing your target audience. It all helps you to have conversations with others to accomplish these tasks.

Here's how to do it:

Be Direct and Personal

Don't post, *"Who wants to help me launch my book?"* Send personal messages or emails. Explain why their support matters and what you're asking them to do.

Show Them the Benefits

People are more likely to help if they know the benefit. Offer them:

- Early access to your book (PDF or print copy).
- Exclusive behind-the-scenes updates on your author journey.
- A shout-out on social media or in your acknowledgments page.

Make It Easy

Give clear instructions: when to buy, where to leave a review, what to share, and even sample social media posts they can copy-paste. The easier you make it for your team, the more likely they'll follow through, and the more powerful your launch will be.

WHAT TO ASK YOUR LAUNCH TEAM TO DO

A simple 3-step request works best:

1. Read the book before launch day (give them 2–3 weeks if possible).
2. Leave a review within the first 72 hours after launch. Early reviews help your book rank better on Amazon and other platforms.
3. Share the book during launch week, whether through a post, an Instagram story, or simply telling their friends.

LAUNCH TEAM REALITY CHECK

Not everyone will follow through, and that's okay. If half of your team does what you asked, you're winning. Celebrate the ones who show up, and don't take it personally if others don't.

I've learned now that this comes with the territory, and you must be okay letting it go, or otherwise you'll find yourself upset frequently.

Many authors get stuck on how to ask for help, so I've included a "Launch Team Email Script Template" in the Resources section to make this easy. Adapt it, make it personal, and send it out with confidence. The point isn't perfection, it's momentum. Even a few active teammates can make a big impact, and that is what matters the most when self-publishing.

WHY EARLY BUZZ MATTERS

Many self-publishing authors don't realize that the weeks leading up to your launch are as crucial as launch day itself. I've heard so many stories about how we focus heavily on the writing and publishing, but fail to think about the promotion part of the process. This is a common oversight. Think of your book like a movie release, trailers, behind-the-scenes interviews, and sneak peeks are what get people excited before opening night. Your book deserves the same treatment.

When I launched Unshaken Leadership, I learned this the hard way. I waited until the book was almost live before talking about it publicly, and while I had great support, I realized I had missed weeks of potential excitement and preorders. By the time I launched my second book, I started dropping teasers, sharing quotes, and even posting pictures of the manuscript, and the difference was night and day.

HOW TO CREATE EARLY BUZZ

How do you avoid the same mistake I made? Let's talk about it and build anticipation the right way.

Through extensive research, including countless YouTube videos, I've gathered insights and strategies that I've personally tested and now share with you.

A few simple ways to get people curious about your book before it's released:

1. Tease Without Oversharing

You don't have to reveal the entire book, only enough to spark interest.

Share things like:

- **Behind-the-scenes updates:** A photo of your proof copy arriving.
- **Quotes or excerpts:** A powerful sentence or paragraph that resonates with your message.
- **Countdown posts:** "30 days until launch, this book will change the way you think about [insert key theme]!"

Self-Publishing Advice: End every post with a call-to-action, even if it's simple: *"Who's excited?"* or *"Want to join my launch team? Message me!"*

2. Use Video (Even If You're Camera-Shy)

Video builds a connection faster than text. Try recording:

- A short clip of you opening your author proof for the first time.
- A 30-second story about why you wrote the book.
- A live Q&A where you answer questions about your writing process.

It doesn't need to be perfect, authenticity wins every time.

3. Involve Your Audience

People love to feel part of the journey. Ask them to vote on:

- **Cover options:** "Which one stands out more, A or B?"
- **Favorite quotes: "Which one should go on a bookmark?"**
- **Launch week giveaways:** "Should I give away signed copies or free coaching sessions?"

When people feel like they've contributed, they're more likely to support you on launch day.

4. Offer Something Exclusive

Give your audience a reason to stay tuned. For example:

- A free downloadable guide or journal page related to your book's topic.
- A bonus video training or behind-the-scenes audio note.
- An exclusive early look at a chapter for those who sign up for your email list.

5. Build Anticipation with a Countdown

Start a **10-day countdown** before launch with daily posts. Each day can share something different:

- **Day 10:** Why I Wrote This Book
- **Day 7:** Sneak Peek Quote
- **Day 3:** My Favorite Chapter Highlight
- **Day 1:** Final Countdown Post ("Tomorrow's the Day!")

Self-Publishing Advice: Your Buzz Doesn't Need to Be Loud to Be Effective. Don't feel pressured to be everywhere or post every day. Consistency beats chaos. Even **two intentional posts per week** can keep people excited if you're giving them valuable, relatable content.

And remember, buzz doesn't always equal sales right away. What you're building now is curiosity and trust. The people who are watching silently today might become your best customers a month after launch.

The key is to stay consistent, stay visible, and stay human. That's what builds momentum.

WHAT NOT TO DO WHEN BUILDING BUZZ

I want to share some common mistakes that can kill your launch momentum. While creating buzz is exciting, there are a few traps that self-publishing authors, myself included, often fall into. Recognizing these during your launch period will better position you for success. Avoid these mistakes so your early promotion works for you instead of against you.

Remember, your launch isn't just about the first week; it sets the tone for how your book performs over the long haul.

By avoiding these pitfalls, you'll give your book a stronger foundation for sustained visibility and sales. Below are examples of what to be aware of when you launch your book.

1. TALKING ABOUT YOUR BOOK TOO LATE

The Problem: Waiting until the last minute to share your book leaves readers with no time to get interested.

Why It's a Problem: One of my biggest mistakes with my first two publications was waiting until two weeks before launch to talk about it. People need time to get excited, plan to buy, and spread the word.

What to Do Instead: Start sharing **4–6 weeks before launch** to build anticipation and warm up your audience.

2. OVERSHARING EVERY DETAIL

The Problem: Posting long excerpts or entire chapters can overwhelm readers.

Why It's a Problem: If people feel like they've already "read" your book through your posts, they may lose motivation to buy it.

What to Do Instead: Share short teasers, powerful quotes, or sneak peeks that spark curiosity, and save the full experience for launch day.

3. BEING INCONSISTENT

The Problem: Posting once and disappearing for weeks sends the message that you're not serious.

Why It's a Problem: Readers will quickly forget your book if they don't see consistent reminders, and your momentum will stall.

What to Do Instead: If you have the energy for one post per week, **do that consistently** rather than relying on random bursts of activity.

4. MAKING IT ALL ABOUT YOU

The Problem: Talking only about yourself or your reasons for writing can turn readers away.

Why It's a Problem: Readers are always asking themselves, *"Why should I care?"* If your message is framed only around "I wrote this book because I love storytelling," they may not see how it applies to them.

What to Do Instead: Shift your language to the reader's perspective: *"This book will help you [solve X problem or feel Y emotion]."* Keep their needs front and center.

5. NOT PREPARING FOR QUESTIONS OR CRITICISM

The Problem: Going public with your book invites questions, and sometimes criticism.

Why It's a Problem: If you're not prepared, tough questions, especially about personal experiences or challenging norms, can leave you feeling defensive or shaken.

What to Do Instead: Be ready to confidently explain your "why" and stand firm in your truth. As a Black author, remember that your voice matters, your story has power, and your integrity will carry you through.

Avoiding these pitfalls will make your buzz stronger, more sustainable, and far more effective when launch day arrives.

Self-Publishing Advice: Buzz Should Build Curiosity, Not Fatigue. Avoid flooding your audience with constant "Buy my book!" posts before it's even out. Mix your promotional posts with personal stories, behind-the-scenes moments, and valuable tips related to your book's theme.

Remember, the goal isn't to pressure people into a sale—it's to invite them into your journey long before they even see the cover. And that leads to another layer of preparation most authors overlook, the emotional side of launching your book.

THE EMOTIONAL SIDE OF LAUNCHING YOUR BOOK

I opened this chapter on a personal note, and I'd like to close it the same way. You must be prepared for the emotional side of writing, and for telling the story behind it. I was recently on a podcast, Let's

Get Uncomfortable with Demetrius Truss, and during that experience, we talked about some deeply vulnerable things.

I thought I was ready. I had rehearsed all the commonly asked questions in my head and felt confident I could handle anything. But as the conversation went on, Demetrius asked questions like, "What was one of the pivotal moments in your book that changed you?" or "What was the hardest chapter to write?" My mind immediately went to some raw places, and emotions surfaced faster than I could catch them.

It was a liberating and powerful moment. But it reminded me of something important: as an author, you must be prepared to handle the emotions your own story will bring up, not only while writing, but when you're sharing it with the world.

WHEN OTHERS READ YOUR STORY

I shared that hitting "publish" is one of the most exciting moments of your self-publishing journey, but it's also one of the most terrifying. This is the moment where your private words, the ones you wrote in quiet rooms, sometimes through tears or laughter, become public. People you don't know will read them. Some will love them. Some will criticize them. And some won't care at all.

You must be ready for all three.

When I launched my debut memoir, I had to sit with myself and ask: *Am I ready for people to know this part of me? Am I ready for them to question my decisions, my past, or my perspective?* And that's a question you must ask yourself, too.

As Black authors, this is even more layered because our stories often carry weight, generational pain, personal triumphs, and cultural truth-telling. There's a vulnerability in putting that on paper, knowing that people will form opinions about you based on your truth. But here's the thing: your story has power.

You didn't come this far to shy away now. You wrote this book because you believed it could help someone, inspire someone, or simply let them know they're not alone. And that's bigger than fear.

As you wait for launch day, take time to center yourself in your "why." Remind yourself why this story mattered enough to put in book form. Your job now isn't to please everyone, it's to stand proud in what you created.

When someone asks you about your book (and they will), be ready to speak confidently about it. Own your message, own your experience, and be okay with saying, *This is my truth, and I stand by it.*

Remember this: the moment your book goes live, you become an author, a storyteller leaving a piece of your legacy. And that's something no one can take from you.

You've faced the reality of sharing your story with the world, now let's make sure you do it without being overwhelmed. In the next chapter, we'll talk about how to avoid the marketing stress that weighs down so many self-publishing authors.

CHAPTER 17
AVOIDING MARKETING STRESS

IF YOU ARE ANYTHING LIKE ME, the word marketing might make you sigh deeply. I've already admitted in this book, I don't love marketing. But I've learned to respect it. Why? Because it's the bridge between your book and the people who need it most.

The truth is most self-publishing authors don't have a massive budget or a marketing team. We're juggling work, family, life, and now a book. But here's the good news: you don't need a massive, flashy campaign to sell books. You need **small, consistent actions** that build momentum over time.

This chapter is about keeping it simple, cost-effective, and doable. By the end, you'll have five realistic strategies, an understanding of why consistency beats "viral," and, for my Black authors especially, a deeper look at how community-based support can amplify your work.

And because I know you need something practical; I've included a "7-Day Social Media Quick Start Guide" in the Resources section to help you build awareness without feeling glued to your phone. I'm all about ensuring you can be successful. You can thank me later with a White Chocolate Mocha from Starbucks (no whipped cream).

In this chapter, I want to keep things simple. Time is limited, but the strategies here will provide insight you can apply immediately or save for your own launch. These strategies have been tried and tested with my own endeavors and my clients. Let's start with a truth that took me a while to learn: marketing doesn't have to take over your life.

What We'll Cover in This Chapter

- 5 Simple Marketing Strategies That Work for Nonfiction Authors
- Why Consistency Beats Big, Flashy Campaigns
- Special Focus: Marketing as a Black Author, Community, Culture, and Representation
- Your Practical Tool: 7-Day Social Media Quick Start Guide

MARKETING DOESN'T HAVE TO BE A FULL-TIME JOB

I spent too much time on my first book, stressing over things that didn't matter, and not enough on what worked. I wanted the big moments, radio interviews, TV appearances, viral posts, but the reality is that most sales came from small, everyday actions. Actions like an organic message to my contact list, asking if they'd be interested in checking out my book. Often, they didn't even know I was an author because they weren't on social media much.

Let me say this clearly: **you do not need to become a social media influencer to market your book successfully.** But you *do* need to be intentional. Marketing is about building relationships, showing up consistently, and giving people a reason to care about your book.

Think of it as planting seeds, one conversation, one post, one connection at a time. Here are five simple strategies that have worked for me (and for many other self-published authors).

5 SIMPLE MARKETING STRATEGIES FOR NONFICTION AUTHORS

The best marketing strategies are the ones you'll do. Forget trying to copy huge campaigns with big budgets, you don't need them. What you need are actions that fit into your real life and steadily build visibility over time. A good strategy gives you direction without draining your energy. It takes the guesswork out of what to do next and turns marketing from something you dread into something you can approach with confidence. When you choose methods that feel natural and even enjoyable, consistency becomes easier, and consistency is what leads to results.

Here are five simple, cost-effective strategies that work.

1. LEVERAGE YOUR PERSONAL NETWORK THE RIGHT WAY

Your first buyers are usually people who already know you, but here's the twist: don't blast your family and friends with "Buy my book!" posts. That's a fast way to get ignored. Instead, make it about them. Share why you wrote the book, the problem it solves, or how it might inspire them personally.

One of the best responses I ever got was when I shared a post saying:

I wrote this book for people who have felt stuck and needed a way forward. If that's you, or someone you know, I hope it reminds you there's always another chapter waiting to be written. That post got more shares than the ones where I announced my book.

Self-Publishing Advice: Ask family and friends to share, not just buy. A single post on their social media can your books visibility.

Why? They may have different audiences, so your book gets in front of hundreds of new eyes. And allow them to post during their own time, as sometimes the organic posts are the ones that get the most traction.

2. SHARE BEHIND-THE-SCENES CONTENT

People love a story, and your journey as an author *is* a story. Share moments like:

- Show your writing space (even if it's messy, it makes you relatable).
- Share a sneak peek of your proof copy arriving in the mail.
- Post a personal reflection about why a chapter means so much to you.

When I posted a photo of me holding the first proof copy of one of my books, my inbox filled with messages asking, *"When can we buy it?"* Why? Because people felt emotionally connected to the process.

Self-Publishing Advice: Take photos or short videos throughout your writing and publishing journey, you can use them later for launch day excitement.

3. OFFER VALUE FIRST, DON'T JUST SELL

Your book has value, but you need to demonstrate it before asking people to buy. Show don't sell. Post tips, lessons, or motivational quotes from your book (and yes, pull real quotes from your manuscript, no making stuff up).

For example, before launching Unshaken Leadership, I shared short leadership lessons from the book for two weeks. Each post gave readers a takeaway they could use immediately, long before they had the book in hand.

Self-Publishing Advice: End every value-based post with a soft nudge, like: "This is one lesson from my book, I can't wait to share the rest with you soon."

4. BUILD RELATIONSHIPS WITH GROUPS AND COMMUNITIES

One of the most overlooked marketing strategies is tapping into groups where your target audience already hangs out. This could be Facebook groups, LinkedIn communities, church groups, book clubs, or even alumni networks.

I've shared my books in leadership networks, and because those groups already trusted me, my posts didn't feel like spam, they felt like resources. These opportunities turned into purchases and speaking engagements.

Self-Publishing Advice: Don't jump into a group and immediately post your book link. Contribute first, answer questions, share helpful tips, and naturally mention your book when it's relevant.

5. GET EARLY REVIEWS THROUGH ADVANCE READERS

Nothing sells a book like social proof. People trust other readers more than they trust your marketing. That's why your Launch Team and ARC readers are gold.

When I published *Oakland Hills, Milwaukee Rivers: A Memoir of Survival, Identity, and Purpose* (Second Edition), I shared early PDFs with a small group of readers who agreed to leave reviews on launch day. Those early reviews boosted credibility and encouraged strangers to take a chance on my book.

It's beneficial to make it easy for your launch team. Send them a direct link to where they can leave a review, along with a reminder of what they agreed to do.

Self-Publishing Advice: Marketing works best when it doesn't feel like marketing. Think of it as sharing something valuable with people who need it. And remember, consistency beats perfection, showing up imperfectly but consistently will sell more books than one big, flashy campaign that you quit after a week.

THE POWER OF SMALL, CONSISTENT ACTIONS

If there's one truth about marketing that I've learned, it's this: **consistency beats perfection every single time.**

When I first started marketing my books, I thought I needed elaborate launch events, expensive ads, and professional PR. But what moved the needle the most was showing up consistently, posting about my book, sharing value, and talking about it whenever the opportunity presented itself.

Think of it like working out. One day in the gym won't get you fit, but 15 minutes a day over time will transform you. Marketing works the same way. A single post won't make your book a bestseller, but **showing up 3–4 times a week** over several weeks will keep your book in front of people until they finally decide to buy.

Here's why this works:

1. **Repetition builds familiarity:** People rarely buy something the first time they see it. Studies show it can take 7–10 "touches" before someone takes action.
2. **Consistency builds trust:** When you consistently talk about your book, people see you as serious and committed, not someone focused on quick sales.

3. **Momentum attracts attention:** The more consistent you are, the more people share, comment, and start conversations around your book.

Having a strategy is only the first step; sticking with it is where the real results come from. That's why consistency matters as much as creativity. In the next section, I'll share some quick wins to help you stay on track and keep your marketing moving forward without burning out.

QUICK WINS FOR STAYING CONSISTENT

Maintaining a consistent posting schedule as you're launching your book is essential. You don't have to post every day, but find a cadence that supports the visibility of your work.

- **Schedule** posts ahead of time (use free tools like Meta Business Suite for Facebook and Instagram).
- **Dedicate** 15 minutes a day to reply to comments or messages.
- **Post** at least one behind-the-scenes moment every week.

When I launched my leadership book, I didn't do anything fancy. I committed to posting twice a week with leadership lessons, photos of me at speaking events, and quotes directly from the book. Over time, those posts were shared by colleagues and landed me invitations for workshops, all from consistent, simple actions.

MARKETING AS A BLACK AUTHOR: COMMUNITY-BASED PROMOTION

Since this book is meant to provide insights for "Black Voices," I thought it would be considerate to share some of my own experience. Marketing as a Black author comes with unique opportunities and, at times, unique challenges. Representation matters. Your book isn't just another product; for many readers, it's a mirror reflecting experiences they seldom see in print. That means when you show up, you're doing more than selling a book—you're giving your community a voice. And that, my friend, is a promise you must deliver on every time.

But here's the hard truth that I've realized: we often don't leverage our communities as much as we could. And this isn't only Black authors, because this can apply to other communities of color. Many self-publishing Black authors hesitate to market because they don't want to feel "salesy" or worry about how people will perceive them. I get it, I've been there. But here's the mindset shift: you're not begging for support, you're inviting people into a movement, into a story that may inspire them, teach them, or change their perspective.

START WITH COMMUNITY-BASED PROMOTION

Here are three powerful (and cost-free) ways to build buzz within your cultural and community networks:

Leverage Cultural and Faith-Based Networks

1. **Leverage** Black churches, sororities, fraternities, and community organizations, which are incredible hubs for support.
2. **Host** a reading, Q&A, or small workshop around your book's topic. (*When I launched my first book, speaking at a local church event sold more copies in one day than an entire week online.*)
3. **Reach** out personally: A phone call or direct message goes much further than a generic post.

Tap into Black-Owned Bookstores & Online Platforms

1. **Reach** out to Black-owned bookstores that actively highlight works by Black authors. Reach out with a professional pitch and emphasize how your story contributes to the cultural conversation.
2. **Connect** with platforms like **Mahogany Books**, **The Lit Bar**, and **We Buy Black**.
3. **Leverage** their newsletters and social media, even if they don't stock your book, they may still promote it.

Show Up Where Your People Are

1. **Attend** local events, art fairs, Juneteenth celebrations, community conferences, and bring your book.
2. **Engage** with Black author Facebook, TikTok, groups, or hashtags like **#BlackAuthorsRock** or **#BlackExcellence** on Instagram. These communities thrive on collaboration, and other authors will often share your posts.

REPRESENTATION AS A SELLING POINT

One of the strongest marketing messages you can carry as a Black author is this: **"Our stories matter."** Don't shy away from saying it. Whether your book is about leadership, trauma, or personal growth, your presence alone represents progress in an industry where less than 10% of traditionally published authors are Black.

While selling a book, you're also contributing to a narrative that tells young readers and aspiring writers, "We belong here too." That's not marketing; that's legacy building.

Self-Publishing Advice: When marketing in community spaces, always lead with value. Offer a free talk, share tips, or give people something they can use immediately.

When you give first, people naturally want to support you, and buying your book becomes their way of saying thank you.

SHIFTING FROM SELLING TO SERVING

I started this chapter by telling you the truth and reminding you that I still hate marketing. But over time, I had to reframe how I saw it. **Marketing is about serving people who need what you wrote rather than begging them to buy your book.**

If you wrote this book to help someone heal, grow, or learn, then every time you share it, you're giving someone access to a tool that could change their life. This becomes service over sales.

Here's the mindset shift I want you to adopt:

- Stop **saying**, "I need people to buy my book."
- Start **asking**, "Who needs what's inside this book, and how can I help them find it?"

Truth moment: If *you* don't tell people about it, who will? And if you wrote your story with honesty and integrity, you should be proud to put it in front of as many eyes as possible.

And yes, some people still won't support you. That's reality. Your worth as a writer isn't measured by likes, shares, or even sales. Your worth is measured by the lives you impact, and sometimes that begins with one person who needed to hear what you had to say.

Self-Publishing Advice: When you feel overwhelmed, focus on one person, literally. Write a post, an email, or record a video as if you're talking directly to them. If your message connects deeply with one person, it will connect with many.

MARKETING THAT FEELS LIKE YOU

Marketing doesn't have to be loud, flashy, or fake. It doesn't even have to feel like "marketing." What it does need to be is intentional and authentic. Every post you make, every conversation you have, every time you mention your book, it's planting a seed.

Don't compare your pace to anyone else's, every book has its own timeline. Some seeds grow fast, others take time. But if you stay consistent, keep showing up, and keep serving, your book will reach the people who need it most. And, personally, this was a reality I had to face many times.

Remember, you didn't write this book to keep it hidden. You wrote it to help, inspire, teach, or leave something meaningful behind. That means being brave enough to talk about it, even when you're tired, because someone out there might need it most.

As we move into the next chapter, we're shifting from short-term promotion to long-term impact. Because after the launch buzz fades, your book still has work to do. **Chapter 18: After the Launch** will show you how to keep your book alive month after month, turning it from a book into an opportunity to grow your influence, your platform, and the legacy you're building.

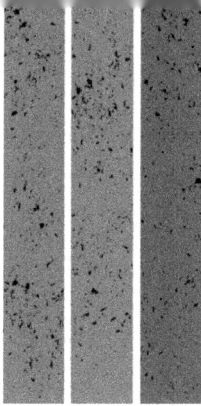

AFTER THE LAUNCH

"Your book's success isn't measured by the first week of sales, it's measured by the legacy it builds over time."

AFTER THE LAUNCH and the buzz fades, you have to silence the noise and decide your next step. Here's a quick story, a secret, that helped me see things differently.

Do you remember when I shared with you that I went into the airport bookstore in Nashville? Yes, I went to check out the bestsellers and see what the book covers looked like, but I also checked how long those books had been out. I picked up every book on the top 10 bestseller list and checked its publication date. Some of the books were three years old or older. And I was shocked.

When I saw that, it gave me reassurance and a reality check: success takes time. The impact of your book may not show up in the first week, or even the first year, but it can still build a legacy.

Keep that in mind during your self-publishing journey because there will be moments when you'll ask yourself, "Is this even worth it?," especially when sales slow down or when your launch excitement fizzles out. But this is where you must position yourself for the long game.

The truth is, writing the book is the first step. The real challenge is selling it consistently, leveraging it to build influence, and keeping it alive in readers' minds—that's where most authors drop the ball. But not you. Not after you've come this far.

This chapter is about keeping your book alive long after launch, growing your readership steadily, and turning it into something that works for you, whether that's speaking opportunities, coaching clients, or simply building credibility that opens new doors.

Now, let's talk about how to **sell for the long game** and make sure your book doesn't fade into the background after its first 30 days. In the next section, we want to answer this question: how do you keep your book visible and valuable after the initial launch buzz? The answer starts with a mindset shift.

THINKING BEYOND THE LAUNCH

Coming into self-publishing, I immediately began thinking about how I could leverage my book to impact my future. I connected it directly to my public speaking platform, **drkeyspeaks.com**, because I knew it was an extension of who I am. You should also start considering what your book could potentially do for you in the future.

Many self-publishing authors treat their book launch like the finish line: hit publish, post the big 'It's live!' announcement, and wait for sales. And for a week or two, they might come. But then the excitement dies down, the comments slow, and suddenly, you're staring at your dashboard, wondering if your book is already forgotten.

As a self-publisher, here is the truth: a launch is not the end of your book's life, it's the beginning of it.

Books that make an impact (and sales) long-term are the ones that remain visible, valuable, and relevant. This means you can't stop talking about your book because the initial buzz fades. You need to think beyond today and ask yourself:

- *How can I keep this book alive six months, one year, or even three years from now?*
- *What opportunities can this book create for me beyond sales?*
- *How can I keep reaching new audiences who need this message?*

If you shift your thinking from selling books fast to selling books consistently, you'll set yourself up for a long-lasting return, not only in royalties, but in influence and opportunities. To answer those questions, here are five post-launch strategies that will keep your book alive long after release day.

LAUNCH STRATEGIES FOR LONG-TERM SUCCESS

1. Keep Talking About Your Book. (Without Being Annoying)

What's the biggest mistake authors make after launch? They go silent. They assume everyone who wanted the book has already bought it. Wrong. New readers are discovering you every single day, and they can only buy your book if you keep it visible.

The key is to keep weaving your book into your content naturally, through lessons, quotes, or personal stories drawn directly from its pages. This isn't about shouting "Buy my book!" repeatedly. It's about showing the value your book carries and letting people see how it connects to their own lives.

Promotional Tip: Frame it as value, not sales. Instead of saying, "Buy my book!" say, "One of the lessons I talk about in my book helped me overcome this challenge...," and then drop a link at the end.

2. Build Evergreen Marketing Habits

Instead of scrambling to "go viral," focus on creating small, consistent habits that keep your book visible over the long haul. Evergreen marketing isn't about chasing trends, it's about showing up steadily in ways that compound over time.

Here are a few simple examples you can start with:

- Post one book-related insight per week on social media.
- Record one short video (30–60 seconds) about a key takeaway from your book.
- Reach out to one podcast, blog, or event host per month to talk about your book.

Think of this as drip marketing, slow, steady, and sustainable. Over weeks and months, these small efforts stack together to keep your book circulating and reaching new readers.

3. Leverage Your Book for Speaking & Authority

Your book is more than a product, it's proof of expertise. Use it as a platform to position yourself as a trusted voice in your field. Every page you've written can open doors to new opportunities beyond book sales.

Here are two of the most effective ways to leverage your book:

- **Speaking engagements:** Conferences, workshops, church events, or community gatherings are always looking for speakers with a powerful message. Your book gives you instant credibility.
- **Media appearances:** Podcasts, radio interviews, or even local TV spots are excellent opportunities to share your story and promote your message while building your brand.

When you position your book as a tool of authority, you're no longer just selling copies, you're building influence, expanding your platform, and creating opportunities that can generate long-term impact.

4. Create Partnerships & Collaborations

Books spread faster when other people talk about them. Partnerships give your message more reach and credibility than going it alone. Reach out to:

- Local bookstores or libraries for readings and signings.
- Community organizations or professional associations aligned with your book's message.
- Other authors for cross-promotions (share each other's books with your audiences).

As a Black author, cultural networks and community-based promotion can be powerful. Churches, fraternities, sororities, and Black professional organizations are great spaces to share your story. Representation matters, your book may inspire someone who never thought about picking up a book like yours before.

5. Keep Collecting Reviews & Testimonials

Reviews are social proof. A book with 50 reviews will almost always outsell a book with five, even if the content is the same. The more readers talk about your book, the longer it stays relevant.

Here are a few ways to keep reviews coming in:

- **Ask** readers for honest reviews months after launch (a follow-up email or DM works).
- **Share** positive testimonials on social media.
- **Offer** incentives, like a bonus resource or thank-you video, for those who leave a review.

Self-Publishing Advice: Don't panic when sales slowdown after launch, this is normal. Think long game and maintain visibility to support ongoing sales.

Keep sharing and your book will grow at its own pace. Some of your most significant opportunities will come months or even years later when someone finally picks it up, reads it, and connects you to a bigger stage.

CLOSING THOUGHTS: PLAYING THE LONG GAME

Your book is more than words on paper, it's a tool that can open doors, build credibility, and create opportunities you may not have imagined when you first sat down to write it. Whether it's speaking engagements, coaching, or simply inspiring someone to take action, your book has the power to work for you long after the launch buzz fades.

Remember: the long game is where lasting impact happens. Stay consistent, keep sharing, and don't measure success only by immediate sales. The true value of your book comes from the influence it builds over time, month after month, year after year.

Self-Publishing Advice: Every time you talk about your book, you're planting a seed. Some will grow fast, others will take time, but if you keep showing up, your story will continue to reach the people who need it most.

After the launch dust settles, some authors stop. But if you want to keep your book alive, you must think bigger. Let's explore how your book can evolve from a single project into a sustainable business.

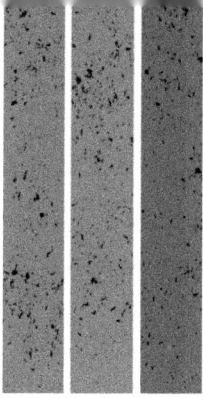

CHAPTER 19

TURNING YOUR BOOK INTO A BUSINESS

**"Legacy is not what you leave for people;
it's what you leave in them."**

"A MILLION BOOKS SOLD!" Is that not something every author dreams of hearing? Moments like that often validate the outcome of being a published author. All over the world, authors like Miles Monroe, Mel Robbins, John Maxwell, and Wes Moore have used books to launch their careers, create speaking opportunities, and gain recognition they never had before.

But what caused it? They wrote to solve a problem.

As I shared at the beginning of this book, problem-solving is what opens doors. Not every author writes with that in mind. Yet when you begin to view your book as a business opportunity, it changes how you see what you produce. It also explains why quality matters, because you never know what opportunity your book might unlock.

How do you position yourself, or your book, to operate as a business? It begins with creating a high-quality product that readers can find and talk about. Beyond that, it means solving a problem the world is seeking answers for and positioning yourself as an expert in your field.

In this chapter, we will cover the importance of writing to solve a problem, how to use your book to teach, the impact it can have on the community, how readers can become advocates for your work, and finally, how to leave a written legacy for generations to come.

WRITING TO SOLVE PROBLEMS

One of the most powerful ways to approach writing a book is to start with a problem and build toward a solution. This works best when you lean into what you already know. What skills come naturally? Which topics do people often seek your advice on? And what needs do you see in the world that people are asking for support with?

For example, Artificial Intelligence is a growing topic in today's world. Many people are searching for help in understanding it, and those who embrace it will be seen as more effective in their work and daily lives. We will talk more about AI later, but the point is this: publishing thrives on three things, entertainment, information, and education. When done well, books provide solutions that meet real needs.

Writing to solve problems not only creates a book but also builds trust and demand. Problems persist, surfacing with each new reader seeking answers. People daily look for help to reduce stress, manage anxiety, balance relationships, grow businesses, heal from trauma, and face numerous challenges. When you offer a solution, readers buy more than pages, they invest in relief, guidance, and transformation.

This is why turning a book into a business is such an advantage. Traditional publishing often looks for "big" books with broad appeal. Self-publishing allows you to target specific problems, niche communities, or overlooked audiences and deliver practical solutions directly to them. It gives you the freedom to write with precision and publish on your own timeline. A single problem-solving book can spark workshops, coaching opportunities, speaking engagements, and even a series of books that expand your reach.

THREE PRACTICAL WAYS TO WRITE PROBLEM-SOLVING BOOKS

Identifying the right problem is just the beginning, and it should be part of the writing process from the start. Earlier, I mentioned that you could write about the sky being blue. If you want to be strategic, that probably would not be your best move, unless something significant happened that made explaining the sky's color essential.

Ponder on this question: how can problem-solving skills translate into authorship? Three of the most effective formats are **eBooks, self-help guides, and journals.** Each provides quick, practical solutions that readers can use right away.

eBooks

Digital books are one of the fastest ways to deliver solutions. They are accessible, affordable, and easy to distribute globally. For authors, eBooks lower the barrier to entry, you can publish more quickly and test how your ideas resonate without the upfront costs of printing. When an eBook solves a specific problem, it can also point readers toward your larger body of work, courses, or speaking opportunities.

Self-Help Guides

Guides are concise, actionable, and designed for readers who want answers now. Instead of covering broad topics, they focus on solving one pain point: how to budget, how to overcome anxiety, how to build a small business, and so on. These guides establish you as a resource and can be bundled with workshops, coaching sessions, or online trainings, multiplying their value as business tools.

Journals

Journals take readers beyond theory and into practice. With structured prompts, exercises, or reflection questions, you help them apply what they have learned in a personal way. Journals are powerful because they create recurring engagement, readers return to them daily or weekly. They also pair well with memoirs, self-help books, or faith-based resources, extending the life of your message while generating an additional income stream.

Taken together, eBooks, guides, and journals show that writing to solve problems is not limited to one format. Each benefits both the reader, who gains a practical solution, and the writer, who builds credibility, multiple revenue streams, and a foundation for long-term impact.

When you write to solve a problem, the next step is to share that solution beyond the page. Books that solve problems often position the author as a teacher. Whether in classrooms, workshops, webinars, or conferences, the lessons from your book become tools to guide others in real time. This is where we turn next: using your book to teach.

USING YOUR BOOK TO TEACH

Your book can be more than a story or a collection of lessons. It can become a curriculum, and for nonfiction authors especially, this is where the real magic happens.

If you have written a self-help, leadership, or memoir-style book, your chapters likely already contain lessons, principles, or reflection points. With some intentional effort, you can repurpose those lessons into workshops, keynote presentations, webinars, or even full online courses.

Before I was an author, I trained higher education professionals for years through webinars. It was one of the easiest and most effective ways to get information to people, no matter where they were. Today, self-publishing authors are using the same approach as both a lead magnet and a revenue stream. Webinars can introduce your ideas to new audiences while also giving you the opportunity to sell coaching sessions, workshops, or companion resources. Online courses take it even further by providing structured learning that extends your message far beyond the book.

When I wrote *Unshaken Leadership*, I did not only want to share leadership lessons. I wanted to create something that could be taught. I pulled key quotes, reflection questions, and examples from the book and used them to design training sessions and presentations. Now, the book is not only something people read. It is something they experience in real time when I speak or teach.

Here is how you can do the same:

- **Pull 3–5 key lessons** or principles from your book and turn them into presentation topics.
- **Create a simple downloadable guide or worksheet** to help readers deepen their understanding.
- **Offer webinars or short virtual sessions** to introduce your content to wider audiences.
- **Expand into an online course** by building modules around your book's key lessons.
- **Speak at schools, churches, or community centers** where your message can connect face-to-face.

Remember, teaching does not mean you have to be an academic. It means you're giving people tools to think differently and act on what they have learned from you. Self-publishing gives you the freedom and control to build these opportunities on your own terms, and teaching through your book is one of the most powerful ways to amplify that impact.

BUILDING COMMUNITY IMPACT

Books can spark movements, but only when they connect with communities that already care about the issues you write about. As a tool for conversation, a book becomes a pathway for healing and collective growth.

For Black authors especially, this carries added meaning. Our stories hold cultural weight, yet they are often overlooked or lost in mainstream spaces. Sharing our stories within our communities preserves culture and heritage while educating others. Representation matters—and so do the spaces where our voices are heard.

For example, while participating in a book club with 15 first-generation students, one reader suggested that I pitch *Oakland Hills, Milwaukee Rivers* (First Edition) as a required reading for one of their cultural classes. It was an idea I had not considered, but the book's alignment with the curriculum, and the connection to my lived experiences, made it a natural fit.

Think about the places where conversations already happen: barbershops, book clubs, churches, community organizations, cultural events, and local festivals. These spaces provide natural entry points for dialogue. Taking the book into those spaces goes beyond marketing; it's about creating connection. You are creating a platform for stories that might otherwise go unheard.

Self-publishing gives you the freedom to decide where and how to share your story. You are not limited by gatekeepers who may overlook or dismiss your message. When you place your book in your community, you amplify its reach and ensure the lessons inside don't sit on shelves but live in the hearts of people. That's how books move from being read to being remembered.

TURNING READERS INTO ADVOCATES

Your most powerful marketing tool is not an ad. It is a reader who loves your book so much that they tell everyone about it. These are your reader advocates, and they can keep your book alive long after launch week.

Turning readers into advocates is simpler than you think. Here's how:

- **Stay accessible:** Respond to reader messages, thank them for sharing your work, and show appreciation publicly.
- **Share their stories:** If someone posts about how your book impacted them, repost it or talk about it.
- **Give them tools:** Share quotes, hashtags, or discount codes that make it easy for them to spread the word.

You are probably wondering, *"How do I use reader advocates from a business perspective?"* Think about it: your readers have access to circles you may never reach on your own. While it may feel a little "market-y," their word-of-mouth is one of the most authentic ways to spread your brand and expertise. All it requires is a little engagement.

Reader advocates turn influence into opportunity by positioning your book as more than a story, linking it to your larger business, like speaking, workshops, or projects. Self-publishing gives you control, making reader promotion more impactful. When readers promote your book, they expand your brand and support your business.

LEAVING A WRITTEN BRAND & LEGACY

The truth is, books outlive us. Long after we are gone, someone may pick up your book, read your words, and feel seen for the first time. That's the power of legacy and the reflection of your brand as an author.

Take pride in this. Your book is not for today only, but also for generations to come. The way you tell your story, the way you package your message, and the level of excellence you commit to will determine whether it's passed down or forgotten.

Every chapter you wrote, every late-night edit, and every risk you took has already planted seeds. You may not see the full harvest yet, but it's growing. Legacy is not built in a day. It is built every time someone opens your book, learns something new, and shares it with someone else.

Using your book as a business tool means treating it as part of your brand and taking pride in what you have created. But to remain relevant, we must also be willing to evolve. As we step into the final chapter, we will explore one of the most powerful tools shaping the future of publishing: Artificial Intelligence, a resource many are already using to extend their brand and build their legacy, but one that some authors are still unsure or even uneasy about embracing.

CHAPTER 20

MODERN BOOK PUBLISHING TOOLS

> "Alright, I vowed in the beginning, to you and to myself,
> that I would be honest and truthful. That doesn't stop now.
> No gatekeeping."

IN CASE YOU'RE NOT FAMILIAR with the term, *gatekeeping* is when people intentionally withhold helpful information or access to resources, often to keep others from advancing or succeeding. That's not what we're doing here.

Our reality is that the world is changing, fast. And whether we want to admit it or not, writing and publishing your book doesn't have to take forever if you have the right tools in your corner.

This book is one investment in yourself, but beyond these pages, there's a whole world of tools and templates that can support your writing, branding, and publishing journey.

This chapter is me pulling back the curtain to share what I've used, real tools that helped me push through writer's block, stretch my creativity, and stay on track. The goal here is to inspire and equip you. And I'm keeping it real with you: this isn't an AI-generated book. What you're reading is built from trial and error, long nights, and lived experience.

Some of these words were typed in the quiet of my home. Others were drafted in the middle of parking lots, sitting on the side of the road, or in the stillness of a gas station corner when thoughts hit me, and I didn't want to let them pass. I did all of that so you can tell your story, boldly, beautifully, and with every resource you need to do it well.

DESIGN TOOLS: MAKE IT LOOK PROFESSIONAL

Because your book shouldn't look self-published, even if it is. Let's talk about design. One of the quickest ways a book gets ignored is if the cover looks like it was made in Microsoft Word, circa 2002. I'm not being funny; but folks are still doing this. Your message might be powerful, but presentation matters.

Think of your cover like the curb appeal of a house. It tells people everything they need to know before they ever step inside, whether you take pride in what you've built or if you threw something together and hoped for the best.

Luckily, some tools can help you make your book look like it came from a traditional publisher, even if you did it all from your living room.

Before we dive into specific tools, let me pause and give you some perspective. Tools won't write your book or magically do the work for you. What they will do is help you present your book with professionalism, save you time, and make the process feel less overwhelming. You don't need to use every tool I mention. Start with one or two that fit your style, budget, and comfort level. Here's the most important part: the best tool is the one you'll use consistently. This isn't about chasing the newest app or trend—it's about finding the resources that support your voice, strengthen your presentation, and help your story shine.

Canva

Canva is like that reliable friend who can help you pull together a whole look without stressing you out. You can design flyers, book covers, media kits, promo graphics, all without needing graphic design experience. I've used it to create my workbook pages, social media graphics, and even slide decks for speaking engagements. Canva Pro gives you access to even more templates and stock photos, but the free version can still take you far.

Placeit

If you've ever seen a clean mockup of a book on someone's Instagram, like a hand holding it or a book on a coffee table, it was probably made with Placeit. You upload your cover, and boom, it puts your book in a beautiful setting. It works for apparel and social ads, too. It's not free, but it saves you a lot of time and makes you look legit.

Book Brush

This tool was made specifically for authors. It gives you 3D book images, ad templates, and even animated book promos. Think of it as Canva's cousin, but trained in publishing. If you're planning a launch and want to create a cohesive look across all your platforms, this is where you go.

Creative Market

Once you get confident, you may want more custom fonts, textures, or branding kits. Creative Market is a site where you can buy high-quality digital assets from real designers. It's great when you want to elevate your brand and not look like everyone else using the same Canva templates.

Unsplash / Pexels

These are free stock photo sites with beautiful, high-resolution images. I use them to find clean visuals for social posts, landing pages, and even book trailers.

QUICK-REFERENCE TOOL GUIDE

Want a breakdown of what each tool costs and where to find them? I've included a **"Price Comparison and Direct Links"** to all these tools in the Resources section at the end of this book.

When using these tools, it's important to maintain consistency. In my own experience, and in working with clients, I've found maintaining consistency to be a common struggle. Choose consistent fonts and colors across your marketing materials to look like a brand, not a hobby.

With so many tools available, it can be overwhelming to know which ones to try first. To make it easier, I've created a quick-reference chart. This chart highlights what each tool is for and why I recommend it, so you can choose the ones that best fit your goals and budget without wasting time or money.

Tool	What It's For	Why I Recommend It
Canva	Social graphics, interior templates, event flyers	Drag-and-drop simplicity, with free and pro features
Placeit	Realistic book mockups, t-shirts, product ads	Polished promotional materials in minutes
Book Brush	3D covers, social ads, print-ready graphics	Made with authors in mind
Creative Market	Fonts, templates, branding kits	Use to elevate your brand beyond Canva
Unsplash / Pexels	Free stock photos	High-quality visuals for social and website use

MARKETING TOOLS: BUILD YOUR AUDIENCE AND SELL SMART

I realize that marketing can feel overwhelming; especially when you're trying to build something from scratch. But don't psych yourself out. These tools helped me stop spinning my wheels and start putting myself in front of the people who needed my story.

Mailchimp

Your email list is your lifeline. I don't care if you start with three subscribers, start. Mailchimp is a great option if you're getting started. It's user-friendly, affordable, and designed for beginners.

ConvertKit

ConvertKit has more automation and is built with creators in mind. It helps you send newsletters, launch announcements, and build long-term relationships with your readers. If you're ready to scale and want more flexibility than Mailchimp, this platform is worth the investment.

Trello / Notion

I used to juggle sticky notes, napkins, and voice memos. Then I found Trello and Notion. These are digital organization boards that let you map out every part of your book launch, from cover design to preorder emails. They help you stay consistent and clear on what's next. I even use them with clients to track their publishing progress.

Publisher Rocket

This tool is a game-changer, though it does come with a cost. Publisher Rocket helps you find the **best keywords and categories** for your book on Amazon. This matters because if your book is in the wrong category, nobody will see it. I use it before every launch, especially when titling my books or updating Amazon descriptions.

Bit.ly / TinyURL

Ever seen those long Amazon links that look like they were generated by a robot? Tools like Bit.ly and TinyURL shorten your links, track clicks, and make your marketing materials look cleaner, especially when you're printing bookmarks, business cards, or including QR codes.

TikTok / Instagram Reels

Do you think these apps are just for teens? Think again. I've connected with readers, authors, and buyers via short videos. I've sold books on TikTok Shop and had thousands watch me read live. If you show up, sharing behind-the-scenes, motivation, or humor, these platforms work. All links and feature comparisons are in Resources.

Tool	What It's For	Why It Works
Mailchimp / ConvertKit	Email lists & launch emails	Email marketing = long-term sales and repeat readers
Trello / Notion	Plan your book release, organize tasks	Keep your head and timelines clear
Publisher Rocket	Research Amazon keywords and categories	Helps you rank and get discovered (paid)
Bit.ly / TinyURL	Short links for bios, print, and promo	Trackable, clean, and user-friendly
TikTok / Instagram Reels	Reach new readers with storytelling videos	Black creators are thriving— this is where readers are

ARTIFICIAL INTELLIGENCE (AI) AND CHATGPT

I have to say this upfront: using artificial intelligence as a tool is innovative, smart, and future-focused. It has the power to revolutionize our work as authors and allow us to get our story out quicker. However, its power lies in how we use it for our benefit. Don't fear it. Embrace it, fully.

AI can help you save time and even money, like checking your sentence structure, analyzing word choice, offering outline ideas, and more. But don't use it to write your book. Doing so risks stripping away your authenticity, and as writers, we can't afford to lose that. Your voice matters too much to hand over to a machine.

Now, I also want to pause and address the elephant in the room. If you've been in author Facebook groups or online writing spaces, you've probably seen the debates. Some people insist that using AI isn't authentic, that it makes your book less "real." I understand where that fear comes from, it feels like we're letting technology step into a space that has always been deeply personal.

But here's the truth: AI is not your ghostwriter, it's your assistant. It won't tell your story for you, but it can help you protect your energy and focus on the parts of writing that matter most. Think of AI like a mirror. It reflects what you give it. The more you share about your tone, values, and even your quirks, the more it can return ideas that align with your voice. You're not replacing authenticity, you're amplifying it.

In fact, self-publishing itself was once dismissed as "not real publishing." Now it's a respected path that has given countless authors a platform. AI is simply the next evolution. Used responsibly, it's not here to erase authenticity, it's here to help you get your story into the world faster, with less stress, and with more focus on the people who need to hear it.

Now let's look at a tool that's genuinely changing the game: ChatGPT. Yes, it's artificial intelligence, but no, it's not your ghostwriter. It's a powerful tool that can help you brainstorm, outline, draft, and organize your thoughts when you're stuck, tired, or overwhelmed.

I've used ChatGPT to generate ideas when I hit writer's block, to refine my book descriptions, and to help me brainstorm launch emails. And I won't lie, it saved me hours. But here's the key: my voice is still mine. I never let AI speak for me. It simply helps me show up.

Because I believe in maximizing every resource available to us, I want to share a few prompt options that have worked for me. These prompts are structured to help you use ChatGPT to support your writing and marketing, not to replace your voice.

Writing Support Prompts

Below are real prompts I've personally used to brainstorm, write, and promote faster, with clarity, confidence, and creativity.

Copy these into ChatGPT. Swap the [brackets] with your info.

- "Outline a nonfiction book for [first-time Black authors] to guide them through writing, editing, and publishing."
- "What are 10 chapter title ideas for a book about [self-publishing success from scratch]?"
- "Give me motivational quotes for authors struggling to finish their manuscript."

Marketing Prompts

- "Write a 150-word back cover blurb for a book about [empowering Black writers to self-publish]."
- "Create three social media captions to promote my book launch on Instagram and Facebook."
- "Draft a TikTok script to explain why I wrote my book and who it's for."

Professional Strategy Prompts

- "What tools can help me design and market my nonfiction book as a first-time author?"

- "Write an email pitch to a podcast asking to interview me about my book [insert title]."
- "Create a bullet-point outline for a lead magnet based on my book to attract newsletter subscribers.

MISTAKES TO AVOID
WITH ARTIFICIAL INTELLIGENCE

Technology can be both a blessing and a curse. Sometimes it seems like it will save you time, but depending on how you use it, it could lead to more stress than expected.

While recording my audiobook, I used ChatGPT to turn my manuscript into a teleprompter script for easier reading. The tool had worked well before when creating content for my motivational videos on TikTok and Facebook, so I assumed it would be as helpful here.

At first, everything seemed fine. Then I noticed the text was being altered according to the software's internal rules. I did not realize it right away, but after a chapter or two, I understood what I was reading was not what I originally wrote. It did not sound like me at all. Some parts were completely off, with phrases I would never use and expressions not aligned with my voice.

Then it hit me. Even though it seemed like I was saving time, I was not. I had to go back and double-check every output to ensure it was accurate and, more importantly, my original work.

Here are some honest warnings you should keep in mind as you start using these tools. They can be powerful when used properly, but they can also cause serious problems if you're not careful:

- **Don't rely on AI to write your book:** This book was written by me, not a robot. ChatGPT is a support tool, not a replacement for your voice. Use it to improve your process, not erase your personality.

- **Don't depend solely on free design templates:** Protect your brand and invest in high-quality mockups or pre-made designs specifically created for authors. You want your book to look as professional as it reads.
- **Don't skip the research:** Use tools like Publisher Rocket, or even study Amazon's bestseller lists, to make smart, strategic choices about your title, subtitle, and category placement. You can write a masterpiece, but if people can't find it, it won't reach the readers who need it.

FINAL THOUGHT FROM THE ROADSIDE

I wrote this chapter while sitting in the parking lot of a 7-Eleven in Illinois, coming back from a Board meeting. At that moment, I knew it would be worth including, because times are changing, and I didn't learn any of this overnight.

The tools and resources I've shared saved me weeks, sometimes even months, in the writing process, and I hope they do the same for you. Much of what I learned came through trial and error, in moments of frustration, and times I wanted to quit. That's why I chose to share them, to help you avoid the same bumps in the road. More than anything, I hope this book has given you the confidence to write your own, even if you're *Self-Publishing from Scratch*. As we reach the conclusion, let's talk about why your story is important and a responsibility to share.

CONCLUSION
YOUR STORY,
YOUR RESPONSIBILITY

When I sat down to write this book, it wasn't about me, or even a personal desire to write a self-publishing guide. It was a book I felt I had to write. I saw too many people publishing without understanding the right structure and format.

In countless Facebook groups, I noticed authors asking the same questions again and again: "I want to self-publish, but I have no idea where to start." "I finished my manuscript, but how do I format it?" "Which platforms should I use?" The need was clear, and the answers weren't. That's when I realized this book had to take precedence, even before my leadership book, my sequel to *Oakland Hills, Milwaukee Rivers: A Memoir of Survival, Identity, and Purpose* (Second Edition), or my projects in higher education. This book came first because it was needed first. And I believe the guidance here can transform lives, create access, and help more voices rise from uncertainty to authorship.

If you've reached this point, I want to thank you for reading, investing in yourself, and believing that your story is worth sharing. Because it is.

Everything we've covered in this book, every lesson, checklist, tool, and personal story, has been about one thing: helping you own your voice and share it with the world in a way that reflects the greatness inside you.

But let me remind you one last time: self-publishing involves more than writing. Writing is only half of the challenge. The other half, the part that no one warns you about, is marketing. You can craft the best book in the world, but if no one knows it exists, your words won't reach the people who need them most.

Writing and marketing go hand in hand, like a marriage, one strengthens and supports the other. If you neglect one, the other suffers.

THE WEIGHT AND POWER OF MINORITY VOICES

Let's also address the elephant in the room, the one nobody likes to talk about. Publishing, whether traditional or self-publishing, remains predominantly controlled by White authors. Research consistently shows that in the U.S., over 80% of published authors are White, while only 5–7% are Black. And when it comes to self-publishing, those figures are even more underrepresented.

Why does this matter? Because our stories, the stories of our people, are powerful, liberating, and essential. They carry history, resilience, and hope that the world needs to hear. Yet too often, those stories never reach bookshelves. Not because they aren't good enough, but because we lack the same access, resources, or confidence to share them with the world.

This is why I stress quality and integrity so much. We don't always get the benefit of the doubt. A rushed, poorly crafted book not only harms your reputation but also perpetuates unfair stereotypes that minority authors "aren't on the same level." But I know the truth, and so do you: our stories deserve to stand shoulder to shoulder with the bestsellers.

Every page you write is an act of defiance against those statistics. Every book you publish with excellence is a statement: *We are here. We are capable. Our voices matter.*

YOUR RESPONSIBILITY AS AN AUTHOR

I wrote this book because I wanted to see more of our voices, strong, polished, and unapologetically authentic, shared in the world. But with that power comes responsibility.

- **Take your time:** Rushed work doesn't hold up over time, and your book will last much longer than the initial excitement of its launch.
- **Respect the craft:** Each edit, design choice, and marketing strategy represents you.
- **Own your story:** Don't dilute it out of fear of what others think. Your truth will connect with the people it's meant to reach.
- **Stand proud:** When your book hits the shelves, you should be able to hold it in your hands and say, "Yes, this is my best work."
- **Don't avoid the marketing part:** Marketing isn't begging for attention; it's serving the people who need your story.

Somewhere out there is a person who will heal, grow, or dream bigger because of what you've written. But they can only experience that if you're willing to talk about your book, post about it, and share it repeatedly.

Write with courage. Publish with excellence. Market with consistency. Let your story stand as proof, to the world and to yourself, that your voice, your experiences, and your message deserve a place on those shelves beside the bestsellers.

Long after the marketing fades and the launch excitement dies down, your book will stand as part of your legacy. Make sure it's one you'll be proud to have represent you, today, tomorrow, and for generations to come.

Here's my last charge to you: Do better. Be better. Share better. You already hold the most powerful tools, your story, your voice, and now the knowledge to publish with excellence. Don't settle for average. The world doesn't need more noise. It needs your truth.

To my Black brothers and sisters, know this: every time you publish, you're reclaiming space in a world that often tries to erase us. You're proving that our voices, our histories, and our imaginations belong in print, on shelves, in libraries, and in the hands of readers everywhere.

When you publish with excellence, you're not releasing a book—you're setting a standard. You're adding to a collective movement, a tapestry of stories that reflect the depth, brilliance, and resilience of our community.

This book is my contribution.
I'm counting on you.
I'm counting on us.

Now go forward, write boldly, and let your book stand as proof that we are here, we are worthy, and our stories will not be ignored.

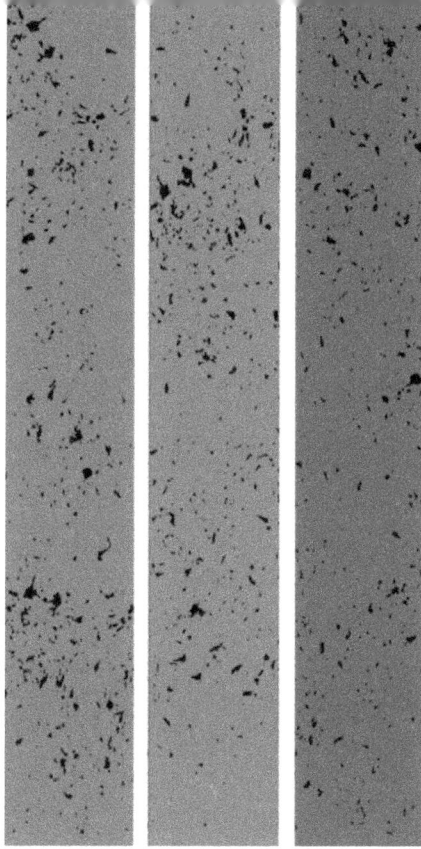

RESOURCES

REPRESENTATION IN PUBLISHING: AUTHORS VS. WORKFORCE

This table highlights the disparity in publishing, both in who gets published and in who works inside the industry. It serves as a quick reference and a reminder of why our voices, our stories, and our publishing choices matter more than ever. Representation shapes which stories are elevated, preserved, and passed on. By choosing self-publishing, you're not only adding another book to the shelf, you're claiming space in an industry that has not always made room for us.

Group	% of Published Authors (U.S.)*	% of Publishing Workforce (U.S.)**
White	81%	72.5%
Minority (All)	19%	27.5%
Black / African American	5–7%	5.3%
Hispanic / Latino	(part of 19%)	4.6%
Asian / Pacific Islander	(part of 19%)	7.8%
Multiracial / Other	(part of 19%)	8.4%

* Source: WordsRated, Author Demographics (2023)
** Source: Lee & Low Diversity Baseline Survey 3.0 (2023)

These statistics reflect data available as of 2023. For updated publishing demographics and resources, visit **www.keywordsunlocked.com**

ADVANCED READER COPY EMAIL SCRIPT

Hi [First Name],

I've got something exciting to share with you, my newest book, [Insert Book Title], is almost ready to be released... but before I make it public, I'm inviting a small circle of early readers to get access first.

Would you like to be one of them?

I'm looking for **ARC readers** to receive a free pre-release digital copy of the book in exchange for an honest review. Your voice will help shape how this book lands when it officially hits the world.

Here's what it means to be an ARC reader:

- You'll receive a **free digital copy** of *[Book Title]* before the public launch.
- I'll ask you to **read the book within 2–3 weeks**.
- If it resonates with you, I'd love for you to **leave a brief, honest review** on Amazon, Goodreads, or wherever you typically read books when the book goes live.

That's it! No pressure. Just your genuine reflections and support.

If you're in, reply with "I'm in for the ARC," and I'll send over your advance copy and instructions for how to share your feedback.

I'm truly grateful to have your support on this journey. This book means a lot to me, and I hope it means something to you, too.

With appreciation,
[Your Name]

ADVANCED READER COPY FOLLOW-UP EMAIL SCRIPT

Hi [First Name],

Just checking in to see how things are going with the advance copy of *[Book Title]*!

I'm incredibly grateful that you agreed to be one of the early readers. Your voice matters, and your review will go a long way in helping others decide if this book is for them, especially as we head into the official launch.

If you've already started reading or finished it, amazing! If you haven't had the chance yet, no pressure at all, I wanted to gently remind you that I'll be gathering early reviews by [insert soft deadline, e.g., "August 15"].

If you're still planning to leave a review:

Here's a quick recap of what to do:

1. Read your copy (digital PDF or ePub)
2. Leave an honest review on [Amazon/Goodreads or platform of your choice]
3. (Optional) Reply to this email with any private thoughts or quotes you'd like me to know

Need a copy of the manuscript re-sent? Just let me know, happy to resend it your way.

Thanks again for being part of this journey. Your support means more than you know.

With appreciation,
[Your Name]

ANATOMY OF A BOOK COVER STANDARDS

WHAT YOU NEED TO KNOW

Before you get too deep into colors, fonts, and images, you need to understand the basic components that make up a book cover. Each part has a purpose, and when done correctly, they work together to tell a story before a single page is turned.

1. Front Cover

This is your first impression, the "handshake" between your book and the world. It typically includes:

- **Title and Subtitle** – Clear, easy to read, and genre-appropriate.
- **Author Name** – Placed prominently (though for some genres, the title takes center stage).
- **Tagline or Hook (Optional)** – A short phrase that intrigues potential readers.
- **Main Visuals or Artwork** – The imagery or design that gives readers an instant feel for your book's tone and content.

Ask yourself: *"Would this make me want to pick it up if I saw it on a shelf?"*

2. Spine

The spine is what most people see first when books are stacked or shelved. A strong spine design makes your book stand out even when only a sliver is visible.

Your spine should include:

- **Title**
- **Author Name**
- **Publisher Logo (Optional for self-publishers)**

Spacing matters, a cramped spine screams amateur, while a balanced spine signals professionalism.

3. Back Cover

The back cover is where the sale often happens. A great front cover grabs attention, but the back cover closes the deal. It usually includes:

- **Book Blurb (Synopsis)** – A compelling 150–200-word summary that teases the story or message.

- **Author Bio (Optional)** – Short and relevant, positioned near your photo.
- **Endorsements or Reviews (Optional)** – Credible quotes that build trust.
- **Barcode/ISBN** – Required for retail distribution.

4. Inner Flap (Jacketed Hardcover Only)

If you're creating a jacketed hardcover, you have two inner flaps to work with. These are prime real estate for:

- Extended Author Bio or Story
- Endorsements or Review Quotes
- Call-to-Action (e.g., website or newsletter sign-up)

Think of flaps as bonus space to build a connection with your reader.

5. Inside Cover (Optional)

For hardcover or high-end print editions, the inside cover can be customized with patterns, graphics, or even a personal message. It's not essential, but it adds a premium feel.

ARTIFICIAL INTELLIGENCE (AI) SHORTCUTS

As a resource to help you build keywords, categories, and product descriptions, which were mentioned in Chapter 15. Copy and paste these prompts into ChatGPT to get useful insights.

Interactive Worksheets & Prompts

Keyword Brainstorm

Write down 10 phrases your ideal reader might type when searching for your book online:

_____

_____

_____

_____

_____

_____

_____

_____

_____

_____

_____

_____

_____

_____

_____

_____

_____

_____

Artificial Intelligence Prompts for Keywords, Categories, and Descriptions

For Keywords:

"Based on my attached manuscript, generate a list of 15 highly relevant keywords and long-tail phrases optimized for Amazon and Google searches. Focus on terms my target readers are most likely to type when looking for a book like mine."

For Categories:

"Based on my manuscript, recommend 5 Amazon book categories (and subcategories) where my book would be competitive and discoverable. Provide a mix of broad and niche categories."

For Product Descriptions:

"Using my manuscript (attached), write a compelling 200-word product description for Amazon using the AIDA formula (Attention, Interest, Desire, Action). Make it emotional, persuasive, and optimized for online book platforms.

AUTHOR WEBSITE ESSENTIALS

Your author website is your digital home base. It's the one place you fully control, unlike social media platforms that can change their rules overnight. A strong website gives readers a central hub to learn about you, explore your books, and stay connected long after they've turned the last page.

The table below outlines the core elements every author's website should have, what to include, why it matters, and a clear action step you can take to set it up right away.

Element	What to Include	Why It Matters	Action Step
About Page	Your story, your "why."	Builds reader connection.	Write a short personal story (2–3 paragraphs) ending with why you write.
Books Page	Covers, descriptions, buy links.	One hub for all your books.	Add your book covers with "Buy Now" links to Amazon or other retailers.
Email Signup Form	Newsletter or "freebie" lead magnet.	Builds your reader community.	Create a freebie (sample chapter, checklist) and connect it to your signup form.
Media/Press Kit Page	Bio, headshot, book info, contact.	Makes it easy for podcasters, bloggers, event hosts.	Upload your author photo and a 100-word bio, make them downloadable.
Contact Page	Email/social links.	Keeps doors open for collaboration.	Add a simple contact form or list your professional email address.
Blog/Updates (Optional)	Tips, behind-the-scenes, or book news.	Boosts SEO and authority.	Post 1 short update a month (book news, lessons, or behind-the-scenes).

BACK COVER BLURB TEMPLATE

SAMPLE BACK COVER BLURB – SELF-PUBLISHING FROM SCRATCH

Have you ever dreamed of writing a book but felt overwhelmed by where to start, or worse, afraid of getting it wrong?

In *Self-Publishing From Scratch: A Practical Guide for Authors to Publish Successfully*, Dr. Keyimani Alford pulls back the curtain on the real journey of self-publishing. With honesty, personal stories, and practical strategies, this book shows you how to share your story without wasting thousands of dollars or sacrificing quality.

Whether you want to leave a legacy, inspire others, or build your professional credibility, this step-by-step guide gives you the tools to write, polish, and publish a book you can be proud of.

Your story deserves to be told. Let's make it happen.

EXERCISE: WRITE YOUR BACK COVER BLURB

Use this framework to draft your blurb:
1. **Hook (1–2 sentences):** What bold statement or question will grab attention?
2. **Reader's Transformation (2–3 sentences):** What will they learn, feel, or achieve after reading your book?
3. **Credibility (Optional):** What makes you the right person to teach or tell this story?
4. **Call to Action (1 sentence):** Encourage them to take action.

Template:
"Have you ever _____? In [Your Book Title], [Your Name] _____ so you can _____ . By the end of this book, you'll _____. Your story matters, start _____ today."

BETA READER SOLICITATION EMAIL SCRIPT

Hi [First Name],

I hope this message finds you well!

I'm reaching out with something exciting, I'm preparing to release my next book, [Insert Book Title], and I'm currently looking for a few thoughtful, honest beta readers to provide feedback before it's finalized.

The book is designed to [insert your book's purpose, e.g., "help aspiring Black authors navigate the self-publishing process with confidence and clarity"]. Since this message is close to my heart, it's important to me that it truly resonates with real readers like you.

Here's what I'm asking from beta readers:

- **Read a draft copy** of the manuscript (delivered via PDF or Google Doc)
- **Provide feedback** on clarity, flow, relevance, or anything that feels off
- Do this within about **2–3 weeks** (I'll provide a simple feedback form to make it easy!)

What you'll get in return:

- A **free digital copy** of the final book
- Your name acknowledged in the **Beta Reader section** (unless you prefer to stay anonymous)
- A sneak peek before the world sees it, and my deepest thanks!

If you're interested, reply to this email with "I'm in!" and I'll send you the next steps. I'd love to have your voice as part of this journey.

With gratitude,
[Your Name]

BETA READER SOLICITATION FOLLOW-UP SCRIPT

Hi [First Name],

I wanted to follow up and check in on your experience with the beta copy of *[Book Title]*. First off, thank you again for being part of this early feedback group. Your insights are incredibly valuable to me as I polish this manuscript for release.

If you've had a chance to start reading, I'd love to hear:

- What's working well so far?
- Is anything confusing or unclear?
- Are there any parts that stood out (or fell flat)?

If life has gotten busy (which I completely understand!), no worries at all, this is a gentle nudge to see if you're still able to share thoughts before [insert soft deadline, e.g., "next Friday, August 9"].

If you need anything from me, like the feedback form link, a resend of the manuscript, or an extension, let me know. I'm happy to help.

Thanks again for walking with me in this part of the journey. I appreciate you more than you know.

With gratitude,
[Your Name]

BETA READER SURVEY QUESTIONS

This survey gathers ratings and feedback from Beta readers on engagement, story flow, emotional impact, writing style, audience connection, and final impressions, plus a demographic section to understand cultural perspectives.

Section	Question	Response Type
Overall Experience	How engaging did you find the manuscript overall?	Rating scale (1–5)
	Did the book hold your attention from start to finish?	Multiple choice (Yes / Somewhat / No)
	In one word, how would you describe the book?	Short answer
Story & Structure	Was the story easy to follow?	Multiple choice (Yes, very easy / Somewhat / No, I was confused)
	Did the pacing of the chapters feel too slow, too fast, or just right?	Multiple choice (Too slow / Just right / Too fast)
	Were there any chapters or sections that felt unnecessary or could be shortened?	Paragraph
Emotional Impact	Which part of the book impacted you the most?	Paragraph
	Did you find the story relatable to your own life or experiences?	Multiple choice (Yes / Somewhat / No)
	What emotions did you feel most while reading?	Multiple choice (select all that apply: Inspired, Sadness, Hopeful, Angry/Frustrated, Encouraged, Other)
Writing Style & Clarity	How clear and easy was the writing style to understand?	Multiple choice (Very clear / Somewhat clear / Difficult to follow)

Section	Question	Response Type
	Were there any areas where the language, tone, or cultural references were confusing?	Paragraph
	Did the author's voice feel authentic?	Multiple choice (Yes / Somewhat / No)
Target Audience & Relevance	Who do you think would benefit most from this book?	Paragraph
	Did you feel represented or seen in the story? Why or why not?	Paragraph
	Do you think the book will resonate with readers outside of the author's direct community?	Multiple choice (Yes / Maybe / No)
Final Feedback	What were the book's greatest strengths?	Paragraph
	What areas need the most improvement?	Paragraph
	Would you recommend this book to others once published?	Multiple choice (Yes / Maybe / No)
	If yes, how would you describe this book to a friend in a few sentences?	Paragraph
	Any final comments, suggestions, or encouragement for the author?	Paragraph
About You (Optional)	Age Range	Multiple choice (Under 18, 18–24, 25–34, 35–44, 45–54, 55–64, 65+)
	Gender	Multiple choice (Female, Male, Non-binary, Prefer not to say, Other)
	Ethnicity / Racial Identity	Multiple choice (select all that apply)
	Religious or Faith Affiliation	Short answer (Optional)

Section	Question	Response Type
	Full Name	Short answer
	Email Address	Short answer
	Payment Preference	Multiple choice (PayPal, Venmo, Cashapp, Zelle)

BOOK PRICING STRATEGY WORKSHEET

GENRE & MARKET RESEARCH

List at least five (5) comparable books (title, author, price, page count, format, etc.)

1. _____

2. _____

3. _____

4. _____

5. _____

PRINT COST & PROFIT CALCULATION

Printing cost per unit: _____

Royalties per platform: _____

Break-even price: _____

READER PSYCHOLOGY & PERCEIVED VALUE

What price would your target audience expect?

_____

What does this price communicate (budget, mid-tier, premium)?

_____

YOUR AUTHOR GOALS

Initial goal: (e.g., *exposure, higher royalties, positioning as a premium expert in the industry*)

Chosen price range based on goal: _____

TESTING & ADJUSTMENTS

Initial launch price: _____

Planned promotional discounts or free promo days?

_____

BOOK PUBLISHER PROS AND CONS CHECKLIST

Amazon KDP	
Pros	**Cons**
Free to use.	Limited distribution outside Amazon unless you use Expanded Distribution (which has restrictions.
Prints books on demand (no upfront costs).	
Global reach via Amazon marketplaces.	The free ISBN reduces professional credibility if you're building your publishing brand.
Option to use a free ISBN.	
IngramSpark	
Wide distribution network, including retail stores and libraries.	$25 change fee per file after the initial 60-day free revision period.
Wide distribution network, including retail stores and libraries.	You must bring your own ISBN.
High-quality print options (hardcovers, dust jackets, different trim sizes).	Slower update times compared to Amazon.
Draft2Digital	
Free to upload, D2D takes a small percentage of sales.	Limited print distribution compared to IngramSpark.
Free to upload, D2D takes a small percentage of sales.	The formatting tool still requires some skill to get professional results.
User-friendly formatting tools (though still require a clean manuscript).	
Great for eBook expansion.	

CUSTOMER SERVICE AT-A-GLANCE CHART

	AMAZON KDP	INGRAMSPARK	DRAFT2DIGITAL
Uploading Your Book	Beginner-friendly and free. Walks you step-by-step through uploading a cover that looks professional.	Professional-level control but less forgiving for beginners. There is a revision fee after 60 days for any changes.	Extremely user-friendly with automated formatting tools, making it ideal for eBooks.
Getting Author Copies	Very affordable author copies can be ordered directly from the Amazon KDP dashboard, but shipping times can vary depending on location.	Professional print quality and wider trim-size options, but author copies are more expensive, and shipping times can be significantly longer.	Print author copies are available, but a newer service. Slightly less consistent turnaround times. However, book quality is good.
Customer Service	Responsive but scripted. Support agents are helpful for basic questions, though they may struggle with complex technical issues.	More professional and knowledgeable about book publishing standards, but responses can take several days to receive.	Known for having some of the friendliest and most responsible support teams in self-publishing.
Audience Reach	Dominates the eBook and paperback market with global distribution through Amazon.com and its international sites.	Wide distribution for eBook and paperback distribution to major retailers.	Known for having an extensive eBook distribution market reach for libraries and online bookstores.

DISTRIBUTION COMPARISON CHART

This chart is a quick-reference guide to help you compare where and how your book can be sold. To use it, start by looking at the "Best For" column to see which platform matches your publishing goals. Then check the royalty rates, upfront costs, and distribution reach to understand the trade-offs. Use this chart to decide whether to publish exclusively on Amazon, go wide with multiple retailers, or combine platforms for maximum visibility.

Platform	Upfront Cost	Royalty (Print)	eBook Royalty	Distribution Reach	Best For
Amazon KDP	Free	60% – print cost	35% or 70%	Amazon only	Fast setup, Amazon focus
IngramSpark	Free	45–55% to stores	40%	Bookstores, libraries, global retail	Authors wanting bookstores & libraries
Draft2Digital	Free	Varies	60%	Apple, B&N, Kobo, libraries	Easy multi-platform eBook distribution
B&N Press	Free	55%	65%	Barnes & Noble	U.S. print & eBook, less global reach

Takeaway: Use Amazon KDP, IngramSpark for wide print distribution, and D2D for wide eBook distribution.

FORMATTING STANDARDS GUIDE

Element	Standard / Requirement
Title Page	Always include: match your cover style; clean, centered, and professional.
Copyright Page	Required in all formats; include ISBN, publisher name, and standard copyright statement.
Dedication Page	Optional: 1–2 lines dedicating the book to someone or a group; a personal touch for readers.
Acknowledgments	Optional: 1–2 pages max; thank editors, beta readers, supporters.
Preface	Optional: personal "why I wrote this book"; used for context before main content.
Prologue	Optional: storytelling hook before the main content; skip for step-by-step guides.
Introduction	Highly recommended: explains why the book matters and what the reader will gain.
Epilogue	Optional: reflective closing or updates; great for memoirs or follow-up content.
Conclusion	Always include: summarize key points and leave readers motivated to act.
About the Author	Always include: professional bio + clear headshot, builds credibility and authority.
Fonts & Sizes	Garamond, Georgia, or Times New Roman (11–12pt) for print, Sans-serif (Arial) okay for eBook.
Spacing & Paragraphs	Line spacing: 1.15–1.5, indent paragraphs, no extra spaces between them.
Indentation	Standard: indent paragraphs, Option: no indent for the first paragraph in nonfiction chapters.
Chapter Titles	Start on right-hand page, centered, bold or all caps, consistent numbering, ⅓-page spacing before title.
Margins & Gutter	Always use official Amazon KDP, IngramSpark, or D2D templates, ensure proper trim size & gutter.
Page Numbers	Include: skip title pages and chapter opening pages.
Headers / Footers	Include book title or author name, consistent placement (header or footer, not both).

GATHERING YOUR IDEAS EXERCISES

EXERCISE 1: WHAT TYPE OF BOOK ARE YOU WRITING?

Write down which category your book primarily falls into and why – if it's a blend, note which one is your focus.

EXERCISE 2: WRITE YOUR CORE PROMISE

By the end of this book, the reader will:

EXERCISE 3: BRAIN DUMP SESSION

Set a timer for 20 minutes and write everything that comes to mind about your book. Don't stop to edit – dump it all out.

EXERCISE 4: CREATE YOUR BUCKETS

Review your brain dump and group ideas into 3-7 main categories. Write them down – these will likely become your chapters or sections.

_____

_____

_____

_____

_____

_____

EXERCISE 5: DRAFT A SIMPLE OUTLINE

Write your chapter titles (or working titles) based on your buckets. Under each title, list 2-3 key points or stories you want to include.

_____

_____

_____

_____

_____

_____

EXERCISE 6: SET YOUR WRITING GOALS

Target word count: _____

_____

Weekly writing goals: _____

_____

First draft completion date: _____

_____

LAUNCH TEAM EMAIL TEMPLATE

Subject: Be Part of My Book Launch Team!

Hi [Name],

I hope you're doing well! I'm reaching out because I have something exciting to share, I'm launching my new book, [Book Title], on [Launch Date], and I'd love for you to be part of the Launch Team that helps get it into the hands of readers who need it.

Here's what being on the Launch Team looks like:

1. **Get an early copy of the book** (PDF or eBook).
2. **Leave an honest review** on Amazon (and other platforms if possible) when it goes live.
3. **Share the book** with your friends, family, or social media audience to help spread the word.
4. **Cheer me on!** (Because honestly, launching a book can feel overwhelming, and your support means a lot.)

You don't have to be a marketing expert or have a huge following, your genuine support and willingness to share matter more than anything.

If you're in, here's what to do next:

Reply to this email with "I'm in!" so I can send you all the details. I'll follow up with your early copy, key dates, and simple ways you can help.

This book means so much to me because [insert 1-2 sentences about why you wrote the book and who it's for]. Having you on this team would not only mean a lot personally, but it will help get this message out to the people who need it most.

Thanks for considering it, I can't wait to share this journey with you!

With gratitude,
[Your Name]

P.S.

Everyone on the Launch Team will get a special thank-you gift from me: [Insert something simple like a signed bookmark, a free PDF guide, or early access to a bonus resource].

LEGAL & IDENTIFICATION RESOURCES

Protecting your work is as important as creating it. Beyond writing and publishing, there are a few legal steps that establish your book as a professional product and safeguard your rights as an author. These resources cover the essentials, from copyrighting your manuscript to obtaining ISBNs and catalog numbers, to protecting your publishing brand and setting up your business identity.

Think of this as the **foundation layer** of your publishing journey: it ensures your book is recognized, protected, and positioned for long-term success.

Resource	What It's For	Why It Matters
U.S. Copyright Office (www.copyright.gov)	Register your copyright.	Protects your intellectual property.
Bowker MyIdentifiers (www.myidentifiers.com)	Purchase ISBNs & barcodes.	ISBN = official book identifier needed for retail.
Library of Congress (PCN/LCCN Program)	Apply for a Preassigned Control Number.	Helps libraries catalog your book.
U.S. Trademark Office (USPTO.gov)	Register logos, brand names, or publishing imprint.	Protects your publishing business name and brand identity.
LegalZoom / Rocket Lawyer (optional)	Access to legal templates and LLC formation services.	Helps authors set up an LLC or business entity for publishing.
IRS.gov – EIN Application	Apply for a free Employer Identification Number.	Keeps business finances separate; useful for tax reporting and royalty income.
Privacy Policy / GDPR Generators (e.g., Termly.io)	Create required website legal pages.	Protects you legally when building email lists or selling books directly.

LEGACY ACTION PLAN: BOOK IMPACT TOOL

IDENTIFY 3 CORE LESSONS OF MESSAGES FROM YOUR BOOK

Why? These are the key takeaways that can be taught, shared, or turned into presentations.

Action Step: Write down three statements that start with:

If readers remember only one thing from my book, it's _____

_____

_____

This story or chapter teaches _____

_____

_____

CREATE A TEACHING RESOURCE FOR WORKSHOPS & TRAININGS

Why? A simple worksheet, discussion guide, or handout turns your book into a teaching tool for workshops or groups.

Action Step: Pull 3-5 reflection questions to appeal to (churches, schools, book clubs, cultural events).

Label It: Reader Reflection Guide or Discussion Questions for [title].

BUILD COMMUNITY CONNECTIONS

Why? Grassroots and cultural networks keep your book alive long after launch and further connect you to the communities it impacts.

Action Step: Canvass where the book's messages fit, where your messages will resonate. Reach out to one place per month to offer a free talk, Q&A, or book signing.

TURN READERS INTO ADVOCATES

Why? Word of mouth is more powerful than paid ads.

Action Step: Create 3-5 shareable quotes or graphics from the book (Canva), post them, and encourage readers to tag you. Respond to every comment or message about the [main theme].

REPURPOSE YOUR BOOK INTO OTHER PLATFORMS

Why? Speaking, podcasts, and articles extend your message beyond the page.

Action Step: Write down 3 podcasts, conferences, or events where your book's theme fits. Draft a simple email pitch: Hi, I'm [Name], author of [book title]. I'd love to share insights about [main theme].

PRE-LAUNCHING CHECKLIST FOR SELF-PUBLISHING

This checklist is designed to ensure you've covered every essential step before hitting that "Publish" button and announcing your book to the world. Print it, check it off, and keep it handy as you approach launch day.

1. Manuscript & Formatting
☐ Proofread & edited your manuscript multiple times (or hired a professional).
☐ Confirmed all formatting is correct (headers, margins, spacing, fonts).
☐ Reviewed and approved proof copies (paper quality, cover alignment, ink smearing).

2. ISBN, Copyright, & Metadata
☐ Purchased your ISBN(s) (if applicable) and assigned them correctly to each format.
☐ Registered your copyright with the U.S. Copyright Office.
☐ Double-checked all metadata (title, subtitle, keywords, categories) for SEO and accuracy.

3. Cover Design
☐ Front, spine, and back cover finalized and checked for errors.
☐ Back cover blurb professionally written and free of typos.
☐ Tested how your cover looks like a thumbnail (important for online sales).

4. Platform Preparation
☐ Created accounts with your chosen distributors (Amazon KDP, IngramSpark, D2D).
☐ Uploaded files and confirmed no template errors or rejection notices.
☐ Ordered and approved proof copies from each platform before finalizing.

5. Pricing & Distribution

☐ Researched competitor pricing to set a competitive, realistic price.

☐ Verified distribution channels (global reach, bookstores, libraries).

☐ Checked author copy order timelines to ensure stock for launch.

6. Marketing & Launch Prep

☐ Built your Launch Team or notified supporters (family, friends, early readers).

☐ Prepared at least **2 weeks of pre-launch content** (social posts, behind-the-scenes, teasers).

☐ Drafted a Launch Day announcement (email & social media).

7. Emotional & Professional Readiness

☐ Accepted that your book will now be public (be ready) for questions.

☐ Crafted 1–2 clear answers for **"What is your book about?"**

☐ Grounded yourself in your **why** – remembering why you wrote this book.

8. Legacy Mindset

☐ Asked yourself: *"If this book is sitting on a shelf 10 years from now, will I still be proud of it?"*

☐ Reviewed for integrity – no shortcuts, no "good enough" mentality.

PUBLISHING & MARKETING TOOLS COMPARISON CHECKLIST

Tool	What It's For	Why I Recommend It / Why It Works	Typical Cost
Canva	Social graphics, interior templates, event flyers.	Drag-and-drop simplicity, with free and pro features.	Free • Pro: $14.99/month
Placeit	Realistic book mockups, t-shirts, product ads.	Polished promotional materials in minutes.	$7.47/month or $89.69/year
Book Brush	3D covers, social ads, print-ready graphics.	Made with authors in mind.	Free • Plus Plan: $8/month • Gold: $12/month
Creative Market	Fonts, templates, branding kits.	Use to elevate your brand beyond Canva.	Pay-per-item ($2–$39 avg.) • Subscription optional
Unsplash / Pexels	Free stock photos.	High-quality visuals for social and website use.	Free
Mailchimp / Convert Kit	Email lists & launch emails.	Email marketing = long-term sales and repeat readers.	Free (limited) • Paid: $9–$29/month (based on list size)
Trello / Notion	Plan your book release, organize tasks.	Keep your head and timelines clear.	Free • Pro Plans: $8–$10/month
Publisher Rocket	Research Amazon keywords and categories.	Helps you rank and get discovered (paid).	$97 one-time fee
Bit.ly / TinyURL	Short links for bios, print, and promo.	Trackable, clean, and user-friendly.	Free • Bit.ly Pro: $8/month
TikTok / Instagram Reels	Reach new readers with storytelling videos.	Black creators are thriving—this is where readers are.	Free

PUBLISHING PLATFORMS CHART

Publishing platforms are the gateways that bring your book to readers. Each one serves a different purpose, some specialize in Amazon visibility, others focus on bookstores, libraries, or global reach. The table below gives you a quick overview of the most common platforms, what they're best at, and why they matter.

Platform	What It's For	Why It Matters
Amazon KDP	Publish eBooks, paperbacks, and hardcovers directly to Amazon.	Largest online bookstore; fast visibility and global reach.
IngramSpark	Print-on-demand distribution to 40, 000+ retailers/libraries.	Reach beyond Amazon; bookstore/library access.
Draft2Digital	eBook aggregator to Apple, Kobo, B&N, libraries.	Saves time; one dashboard = multiple stores.
Lulu	Print-on-demand for workbooks, journals, specialty formats.	Flexible for spiral-bound, photo books, and unique projects.
Smashwords (via Draft2Digital)	eBook distribution to niche and library markets.	Useful for coupons, niche promo, and indie-first audiences.
BookBaby	Full-service publishing (eBook, print, distribution, and design).	More expensive but turnkey "done-for-you" model.
Blurb	High-quality print books, photo books, and art projects.	Best for visually driven books (art, photography, cookbooks).
StreetLib	Global self-publishing platform with wide international distribution.	Expands reach into European, Latin American, and emerging markets.
Kobo Writing Life	Direct publishing to Kobo's eBook platform.	Popular in Canada, Europe, and Asia; strong library distribution.
Apple Books for Authors	Publish directly to Apple's bookstore.	Reaches millions of iOS readers with higher royalty potential.

SELF-EDITING CHECKLIST

Before you hire a professional editor, use this guide to revise your manuscript with clarity, consistency, and confidence.

1. Content Clarity & Structure
☐ Does each chapter have a clear purpose or takeaway?
☐ Are your main points or lessons easy to follow?
☐ Have you removed unnecessary repetition or off-topic tangents?
☐ Is your book organized logically (beginning, middle, end)?
☐ Do transitions between sections and chapters feel smooth?

2. Voice, Tone & Reader Engagement
☐ Does your voice sound authentic, consistent, and relatable?
☐ Are you speaking to the reader, not at them?
☐ Are you using "you" or "we" when appropriate to create connection?
☐ Have you included reflection moments, questions, or prompts (if applicable)?
☐ Are you balancing inspiration with instruction or insight?

3. Grammar, Punctuation & Sentence Flow
☐ Are your sentences clear and concise?
☐ Have you eliminated run-on sentences or fragments?
☐ Did you fix common grammar issues (their/there, it's/its, affect/effect)?
☐ Have you varied sentence length and structure for flow?
☐ Is your punctuation used correctly (commas, semicolons, quotation marks)?
☐ Did you avoid overusing filler words like "just," "that," "really," or "very"?

4. Formatting & Style Consistency

- ☐ Are headers and subheaders consistently styled (font, size, spacing)?
- ☐ Are you consistently using U.S. or U.K. spelling, not both?
- ☐ Are your bulleted or numbered lists styled the same way throughout?
- ☐ Is your paragraph indentation and spacing consistent?
- ☐ Are you italicizing book titles, thoughts, or internal emphasis correctly?
- ☐ Is your use of bold text intentional and sparing?

5. References to Other Works or Resources

- ☐ Are all quotes or statistics properly attributed or cited?
- ☐ Are book titles, resources, or websites consistently formatted?
- ☐ If referring to your own previous books, do you use the correct title and tone?
- ☐ Have you included page or section references if you mention tools inside your book (e.g., "See 'Gathering Your Ideas' in the Resources section")?

6. Final Polish

- ☐ Did you read the entire manuscript *out loud* (or use text-to-speech)?
- ☐ Did you take a break before doing your final review?
- ☐ Did you run a spellcheck *and* grammar check (Grammarly, ProWritingAid, Word)?
- ☐ Have you checked your Table of Contents against your chapter titles?
- ☐ Is your manuscript ready for formatting (no tracked changes, comments, or placeholders left)?

TOOL COMPARISON TABLES – ISBN OPTIONS AND MARKETING PLATFORMS

This chart is designed to help you quickly evaluate the most common publishing tools, without getting lost in the noise. Start by scanning the "Best For" column to see which tools match your stage of publishing (first-time author, brand builder, or pro). Then weigh the costs, strengths, and weaknesses to determine what aligns with your goals and budget. Remember, you do not need every tool, choose what makes your publishing journey smoother, not more complicated.

ISBN Options

Option	Cost	Pros	Cons	Best For
Free Amazon KDP ISBN	Free	No cost, quick	Amazon listed as publisher	Budget-conscious authors
Bowker ISBN	$125 one / $295 ten	Author owns imprint	Costly upfront	Authors building a brand
IngramSpark ISBN	Free	Used outside Amazon	Still shows IngramSpark as owner	Print-focused authors

Marketing Platforms

Platform	Cost	Strengths	Weaknesses	Best For
Amazon Ads	Flexible	Targets buyers on Amazon	Learning curve, cost risk	Direct sales push
Facebook Ads	Flexible	Great for brand-building, wide reach	Cold traffic, higher spend	List building, awareness
Book Bub Ads	Flexible	Readers already buy books	Expensive clicks	Genre-specific targeting

ACKNOWLEDGMENTS

Thank you, life.

You have taught me so many valuable lessons, more than I can count. There have been highs and lows, sleepless nights, and bold risks I've taken to reach this point. But each moment played a significant role in getting me here.

This book was written in my room over the course of many summer weekends, while the sun was shining, temperatures soared above 70 degrees, and festivals filled the parks and streets of Milwaukee. Yet I stayed inside, because a purpose was burning in my heart: to create something meaningful for my community, a guide to help us publish our stories with excellence and pride.

Like you, the reader who purchased this book, I once searched for guidance on how to publish. That pursuit opened the door to understanding the intricate nuances of this industry. I soaked up knowledge like a sponge, determined to get it right. So, thank you, life, for showing me some of the most valuable lessons come when you choose to learn them yourself, without waiting for someone to hand them to you.

Although anyone can use this book to sharpen their writing and self-publishing skills, I wrote it specifically for Black aspiring authors, to address the racial disparities that persist in this field. We don't have to live in a box, think in a box, or write in a box. But when it comes to publishing, we do need to operate within the industry's standards to be seen, respected, and remembered. Now that we know better, we must do better.

To my friends, thank you. Your willingness to listen, let me bounce around ideas, and say, "That's a good idea," or not, gave me the momentum I needed most.

To my clients, thank you for trusting me with your stories. Your courage, your questions, and your commitment taught me just as much as I guided you. Your journeys helped shape the purpose of this book.

And above all, thank you, God, the One who awakened gifts I once buried and who continues to push me to lead, create, and serve with purpose. I am in awe of what You've done, what You continue to do, and what You are preparing for the future.

ABOUT THE AUTHOR

Dr. Keyimani Alford is an author, speaker, and founder of Keywords Unlocked Publishers, a Black-owned publishing company where he helps aspiring writers turn their stories into professional, high-quality books. With a passion for helping people find healing and purpose through storytelling, Dr. Alford guides self-publishing authors, especially those from underrepresented communities, in sharing their narratives with excellence and authenticity.

In addition to his publishing work, Dr. Alford is a seasoned higher education leader with over two decades of experience supporting student access, success, and equity. His books and teaching are grounded in one mission: to empower others to reclaim their voice, inspire change, and leave a legacy through the power of words.

ADDITIONAL PUBLICATIONS BY KEYIMANI ALFORD

Self-Publishing from Scratch: A Practical Guide
for Authors to Publish Successfully with Insights for Black Voices

Oakland Hills, Milwaukee Rivers
A Memoir of Survival, Identity, and Purpose (Second Edition)

Unshaken Leadership: A Practical Blueprint for Overcoming
Challenges, Learning from Mistakes, and Growing in Confidence

Other Workbooks and Journals

Oakland Hills, Milwaukee Rivers (First Edition)

Oakland Hills, Milwaukee Rivers Workbook
A Guide for Faith and Biblical Application

The Healing Companion
A Guided Journal for Reflection, Resilience, and Becoming

Keywords Unlocked Ultimate Motivational Planner
A Guide to Accomplishing Your Goals